NEW MILTON LIBRARY
26. MAR 02
Tel: 613
05. NOV
04. MAR 96
30. JAN 97
09. OCT 97
25. FEB 97
20. JUL
01. JUN 00
NOV 00
DEC 00
22. NOV 01.

SCOTLAND YARD'S COCAINE CONNECTION

SCOTLAND YARD'S COCAINE CONNECTION

Andrew Jennings
Paul Lashmar
and Vyv Simson

JONATHAN CAPE
LONDON

First published 1990

Jonathan Cape Ltd, 20 Vauxhall Bridge Road, London SW1V 2SA

A CIP catalogue record for this book
is available from the British Library

ISBN 0–224–02521–X

Typeset by Selectmove Ltd, London
Printed in Great Britain by
Mackays of Chatham PLC

CONTENTS

ILLUSTRATIONS

Photographs supplied by Emma Cattell, Frank Chambers, David Modell, London News Service, News International, Press Association and H.M. Customs

1 · HOSTILE FORCES

FEW WOULD SPARE a second glance for the plump, bespectacled, middle-aged figure of Nikolaus Chrastny as he makes his way through the streets of London or New York, Munich or Miami. He is a master of disguise, and he needs to be, for Chrastny is one of the most wanted men in the world. Since 1973, when the West German police issued an international warrant for his arrest for his part in a jewel robbery, he has been a fugitive, sought by police forces throughout Europe and the Americas. During his years on the run Chrastny has based himself in Florida, perfecting his skills as one of the world's top cocaine smugglers. There are two reasons why he has evaded capture for so long. He is a brilliant organiser but, more importantly, he relies on the help of corrupt officials and detectives in every operation he carries out.

Special Agent Mike Minto also escaped to Florida, but for more honourable reasons. He took with him a pension, earned for 20 years work in the New York State Police Department, where he confronted organised crime and racketeering. By 1979 he'd had enough of New York's capricious climate and of the interminable paperwork and never-ending office politics that went with the rank of Captain. Minto headed south for the Sunshine State and back to the basics of detective work, out on the streets of Florida fighting the ever-growing cocaine trade.

In the summer of 1984, Minto and his younger and studiously polite partner, Mike Breece, one of the few special agents in the service who could boast that he was Florida born and bred, launched a secret investigation. They code-named it 'Operation Internos' and it soon grew beyond the borders of Florida and in time spread to California and nearly every state of the union. Then it leapfrogged the Atlantic and drew in law enforcement agencies in Britain and across mainland Europe.

Dozens of determined detectives around the world united with one aim: to intercept the biggest ever cocaine shipment from Colombia to Europe — a consignment they believed could weigh as much as three-quarters of a ton — and to arrest the team who had been planning their coup for nearly two years. Eventually this unique investigation resulted in a little of the cocaine being seized and a few of the gang going to jail.

But the investigators were outmanoeuvred at nearly every turn. They found it impossible to get the result they deserved. Only later did they discover that, from the very beginning, their efforts had been sabotaged. There was a traitor in their ranks.

In the summer of 1986 Chrastny slipped out of Florida and made his way to Colombia for a crucial meeting with his suppliers. Once the arrangements had been completed, he flew to Britain. Chrastny was now near to completing the most ambitious project of his criminal career — smuggling the largest quantity of cocaine ever known to arrive in London.

A month later, on the morning of 20 August, Chrastny could be found sitting in the passenger seat of a Cessna light aircraft on the runway of Plymouth's Roborough Airport. Shortly after 9 am the control tower gave clearance for take-off and within minutes the little plane was out over the Atlantic coast. Through his binoculars Chrastny soon spotted what he was searching for. Approaching the estuary of the Helford River in Cornwall was a catamaran, the *Katlyn*, which had been chartered ten days earlier by one of Chrastny's lieutenants.

On Brian Van der Breen's business card was the impressive title of 'Location Manager, Middle Latitude Films Inc.' The bearded American had claimed that he wanted to use the *Katlyn* for filming along the south-west coast of Britain, but on that particular morning Van der Breen was engaged in something more sinister than looking for attractive aspects of the Cornish cliffs. Under the cover of darkness, Van der Breen and his crew mate, Martin Schreiber, a lanky German neo-fascist, made a dangerous rendezvous in the Western Approaches with a much larger boat, the *Aquilon*.

Chrastny had bought the former North Sea pilot vessel a year earlier in Greece. On the morning of 20 August, 1986, concealed in specially built compartments in the *Aquilon*'s fuel tanks, was over £100 million worth of Colombian cocaine.

The *Aquilon* had begun her smuggling run to England from the Christobal Yacht Club in Panama six weeks earlier, on 4 July, American Independence Day. The 392 kilos of cocaine on board were supplied by the Colombian Ochoa family, one of the four big names that make up the notorious Medellín drug cartel. Nikolaus Chrastny had made the deal personally with 'Uncle Alberto' Ochoa, paying $190,000 in cash for 38 kilos of the drug and taking the rest on credit. A credit line of such magnitude with the Ochoas made it clear that this was by no means Nikolaus Chrastny's first cocaine deal.

Towards the end of her voyage the *Aquilon* was in regular radio contact with the *Katlyn* berthed at Falmouth, informing Van der Breen and Schreiber of her progress and endlessly checking and rechecking the plans to get their criminal cargo ashore. At around 2 am on 20 August the *Aquilon* passed the Lizard and, feigning engine trouble, cast anchor. The *Katlyn*, newly equipped with a sophisticated navigation device which could pin-point the exact location of the *Aquilon*, turned into the wind 150 yards short of the larger vessel.

Van der Breen and Schreiber waited. Suddenly, out of the darkness, came a Zodiac rubber dinghy. It was piloted by Eggert Kronby, the Danish master of the *Aquilon*, who had with him two heavy-duty plastic sacks. The three men heaved the sacks, heavy with cocaine, out of the dinghy and into the catamaran. The transfer had taken just five minutes.

Six hours later Nikolaus Chrastny, strapped safely into a passenger seat in the Cessna, was gazing down at the *Katlyn* as she made for an anchorage buoy in the Helford River. From there the cocaine would be split up into smaller loads for delivery to his London distributor. From his airborne position Chrastny made radio contact with *Katlyn* and told the smugglers that there were no special police activities on the radio frequencies he was monitoring, and that from his position he could see 'no hostile forces'.

Chrastny had taken elaborate precautions to evade the British Customs and Excise officers whose task is to prevent drugs being landed along the British coast. It was the most dangerous stage of the operation and he was acutely aware of the risks of interception and capture at sea. Once the drugs were ashore and the distribution had begun Chrastny could relax, safe in the knowledge that he had a unique insurance policy against being arrested by the police. He had been given the guarantee he wanted at the start of the conspiracy two years earlier. Chrastny's partner in the cocaine conspiracy, Britain's top gangster, had assured him that they would have an inside man protecting them at Scotland Yard.

As the *Katlyn* and her cargo of cocaine hove to in the Helford River, working parties of convicts were setting out for their morning labours 300 miles away at Wayland prison in Norfolk. One of them, the stocky, balding figure of gangster Roy Garner, was on edge as he waited restlessly for the message which would tell him that, despite his incarceration, the foot soldiers of his criminal empire had pulled off another major coup.

Garner was nearing the end of a three-year sentence for stealing nearly £2 million in a tax fraud but, with only three months left to serve, he was itching to be back on the streets of London organising what he planned to be his most lucrative coup in 20 years of crime — the distribution of the 392 kilos of Colombian cocaine he had agreed to buy from Nikolaus Chrastny.

Being locked up in jail at the crucial moment was more than just inconvenient for Garner. The fraud sentence had upset everything. Having gone to great pains over the years to arrange protection from corrupt police officers, he expected to avoid going to prison. Now in his mid-forties, he had enjoyed millionaire status for a decade. He had interests in night clubs, property and race horses. His luxury town house was Cannon Lodge in an expensive part of North London and his country home a stud farm with 200 acres of prime land in the heart of the English Home Counties. Garner took holidays at his £250,000 seafront apartment in the exclusive Hampton Beach Club on Florida's east coast. He drove a gold Mercedes, sailed a yacht, owned two family homes, with a 'Mrs Garner' and offspring installed in each. He also kept a young mistress. For Roy Garner, crime paid.

Is Roy Garner a brilliant criminal or only Britain's most cosseted crook? The truth will never be known; the facts are easier to grasp: despite Garner's horrific career of crime spanning two decades, Scotland Yard went out of its way to ensure that he never suffered a single day in jail. The protection and favours made available to Garner were on offer from the top to the bottom of the Metropolitan Police. Decent detectives who tried to beat the system and arrest him believe they were continually blocked. So it is impossible to judge whether Garner was one of Britain's cleverest criminals — or just the most protected. Only when Garner was unwise enough to operate outside the jurisdiction of Scotland Yard and strayed into areas policed by Customs and Excise investigators, was he caught and jailed.

Unhampered by fear of interference from the Metropolitan Police Garner grew in power and influence over both London's criminal underworld and the rank and file detectives. By the early 1980s a secret Scotland Yard report stated bluntly that he was 'in the forefront of major crime'. A couple of years later a recently retired senior Yard detective went on the record and defiantly denounced Garner as 'the Overlord of crime in London'. That detective was one of many who, having tried to penetrate the charmed circle of protection around Garner, referred to him despairingly as 'The Untouchable'.

Garner's intelligence file at Scotland Yard states that from the late 1960s he was a major criminal, extremely active in the fashionable crimes of the day. His first fortune was created at the point of a sawn-off shotgun as he led his troops in attacks on security trucks and payrolls. The mountain of cash seized in 'across the pavement' raids was then invested in long firm frauds, which operated like a con artist's 'sting'. The front company would place huge orders with its wholesalers and then the goods — all on credit — would be spirited away long before the unsuspecting suppliers discovered that their customer had shut up shop and disappeared.

Garner also became one of London's leading 'Fagins', using his cash flow to acquire stolen property — everything from gems to lorryloads of whisky — from the capital's thieves. He moved with the times and celebrated Britain's entry into the European Community by joining the fraudsters who ripped off millions of pounds in VAT rackets. He got away with nearly £2 million, but it was his first mistake. Garner was efficiently gathered up by Customs officers and dispatched to Wayland prison. Yet his maximum jail sentence was a close-run thing.

Spectators at the Old Bailey for his sentencing were surprised to see a senior Scotland Yard officer outside the court. They would have been even more taken aback if they had known his mission. He was bearing a secret letter from the Yard pleading for leniency for Garner.

Scotland Yard has two quite separate files on Garner. One, kept in the Criminal Intelligence department, lists his appalling crimes over the decades, the other is locked away from prying eyes in the safe of the Deputy Assistant Commissioner for Specialist Operations on the Yard's fifth floor. It has to be kept secure because it is the history of Garner's second role in the world of major London crime — as Scotland Yard's top informant.

Under the code-name of 'Dave Granger' he is credited with giving information that has led to the arrest and jailing of hundreds of London's criminals and the recovery of millions of pounds' worth of stolen property. The entries in this file are a history of betrayal. They list secret meetings over the years between Garner and his Scotland Yard contact and the criminal names that he gave, the crimes they had committed and the whereabouts of the missing cash or property.

Garner's motives were never altruistic: he had identified yet another way to make money out of crime. Informing can be a lucrative business and, backed by the Metropolitan Police, Roy Garner was paid nearly a quarter of a million pounds in rewards from insurance companies during one twelve-month period alone. Even now, he is still hoping to receive further rewards totalling nearly £3 million.

The set of intelligence files that lists Garner's crimes is a sordid inventory of armed robberies, frauds and drug dealing. The other, secret files in the DAC's safe bulge with memos praising the criminal. Most of them have been written by one man, Detective Superintendent Tony Lundy. From the mid-1970s Lundy was Garner's Scotland Yard handler, and it was through Lundy that Garner channelled information about his fellow criminals and their crimes. Despite the overwhelming evidence in the Criminal Intelligence office about Garner's crimes, and Lundy's reputation as a detective with an unrivalled knowledge of crime in the capital, he seemed unaware of the extent of Garner's activities. Indeed, he went so far as to write a letter to his bosses championing Garner's plea that he is not a major criminal, only a victim of other, unscrupulous, informers.

Tony Lundy, known to his subordinates as 'Top Man', is an ambitious, blunt and calculating Lancastrian. He boasts, 'I have been one of the most successful detectives the Metropolitan Police has ever employed. I have been responsible for the recovery of more property and cash during my career than any other detective. Anyone would be entitled to be proud of that record and to have earned the respect of senior officers.' In his 27 years of service Lundy received 23 commendations from successive Police Commissioners and Old Bailey judges, pioneered a new method of police investigation through the use of multiple supergrasses and was paraded before the public as proof that the Metropolitan Police were 'winning the war against crime'.

Other Scotland Yard officers were less enthusiastic about Lundy. They investigated his relationship with Garner and the result was a confidential memo, written by Scotland Yard's most senior internal investigator, which states unequivocally what many other experienced officers had long suspected — that 'Mr Lundy is a corrupt officer'. Lundy disputes this, claiming a conspiracy against him and pointing out that, at the time, no specific evidence was produced to justify the allegation.

Both Garner and Lundy prospered from their secret dealings. Garner, seemingly immune to prosecution, embarked on increasingly ambitious and rewarding crimes. Tony Lundy, cracking case after case, became more powerful and climbed the ladder of Scotland Yard's elite squads. Despite almost continuous internal investigation, Lundy's relationship with the 'Overlord' of London crime could not be broken.

In Florida the narcotics cops and their Operation Internos continued. Eventually one of Chrastny's associates cracked: he told Minto and Breece that he would give evidence against the rest of the gang and also name the allegedly crooked detective inside Scotland Yard. In California both the US Justice Department and the Los Angeles Homicide Squad uncovered more of the same allegations. In Wiesbaden the German drugs police painstakingly tracked down information about the missing

Chrastny. In London Customs officers launched 'Operation Redskin', arrested the German and Roy Garner and seized 50 kilos of the cocaine. Chrastny decided to co-operate and made a statement naming the alleged gang member inside Scotland Yard who was going to tip them off if investigations into the drugs plot began. He went on to confirm that the gang had indeed been warned that they were under surveillance. He agreed to give this crucial evidence in court. Shortly afterwards, Chrastny escaped from a high-security cell and has never been seen since, although he occasionally contacts the German media. The British press speculated whether he had been helped to escape by corrupt detectives at Scotland Yard.

By the time Roy Garner was brought to the Old Bailey, in March 1989, accused of smuggling the largest known consignment of cocaine into Britain, Tony Lundy had hastily retired from the police on grounds of 'illhealth'. However, he made a speedy recovery and two months later came to the court as a defence witness for Garner. Lundy had to begin his evidence by strenuously denying prosecution allegations that had made headlines in every paper; that he, Tony Lundy, was the cocaine gang's inside man. He went on to list the commendations he had won in his career as a police officer. The rest of his evidence will never be known because it was delivered in secret. Anyone who dared to publish the explanations Lundy gave when the prosecution accused him of being the gang's inside man would face immediate imprisonment for contempt of court. In a remarkable decision, which the Judge himself declared was 'repugnant and exceptional', the press and public were ejected from the court after half an hour and Lundy was allowed to give the majority of his evidence on behalf of Garner *in camera*. In Britain such secrecy is usually confined to cases where national security is involved. There were no national security aspects to this case. Whatever he tried to say on Garner's behalf, Lundy's secret evidence failed to impress the jury of seven women and five men. They returned a unanimous verdict of guilty. Judge Machin told Garner that he was an 'evil man' and jailed him for 22 years.

Outside the court Lundy proclaimed that he would rather have given his evidence in public and that he 'never had anything to hide'. He insisted that both judge and jury had got it wrong. Roy

Garner was innocent and the case was the result of a vendetta against the Metropolitan Police by Customs and Excise officers. Lundy also claimed that he himself had been the subject of 'irresponsible, unsubstantiated and scandalous' allegations from an alliance of criminals, Freemasons and journalists. 'I have had nothing but rumours of corruption, allegations that I took bribes, that I bent evidence, that I protected supergrasses from long sentences — all without a shred of evidence to back it up.'

In an 'exclusive' article in a British tabloid the following Sunday, Lundy went on in the same vein: 'If only the powers that be had given me the £2 million or thereabouts that was spent on internal investigations against me, I could have cleared up half the world's crime.' The article appeared under the banner headline 'Bent or Brilliant?' As Tony Lundy started his enforced retirement from the Metropolitan Police and Roy Garner his 22 years in prison, a most remarkable chapter in the history of Scotland Yard came to an end. The story, however, is far from over.

2 · THE OVERLORD

THE GANG LEADER, his face blurred behind the stocking mask, wrenched open the driver's door. 'Get out and you won't get hurt,' he bellowed. Sensibly, the guards did not resist him or the three others robbers and their sawn-off shotguns. They were bundled into a waiting van and their security truck was driven away, its cargo of gold bars and precious stones lost for ever.

It was one of the most audacious acts of banditry carried out on London's streets. The team of robbers ambushed a KLM Airlines armoured truck as it drove from Piccadilly down into the Hyde Park Corner underpass at the peak of the evening rush hour, bound for Heathrow airport. They left one van sprawled across the road to block off pursuit and then spirited the truck away to an empty warehouse in Paddington. The guards never had a chance; they screamed into their radio for help as the robbers closed in but the signals bounced back from the concrete all around them. The haul of £117,000, a huge one in December 1970, was sold off through the dealers of Hatton Garden within days.

It was a personal coup for the gang leader who had organised such a precise, surgical assault; Roy Garner had arrived at the top of London's criminal big time. Nearly two decades would pass before he was toppled. In a prison visiting room many years later we asked an armed robber, halfway through a

25-year sentence, where Garner learned the trade of gunman. 'Working in the meat market, that's enough,' he laughed.

Roy Garner was not brought up with a shotgun in his hand. He was born on the eve of World War Two, one of four children from a respectable working-class Holloway family. As was the custom, he followed his father to work as a porter at Smithfield meat market but then he changed course and was apprenticed to his uncle Johnny Garner, who had a successful shopfitting business. The turning point came when Roy met Kenny Ross. Ross had come up through a harder school and would spend time in Dartmoor. When Garner met him Ross was already active at lorry hijacking. He was known in the trade as a 'jump-up artist': the man who makes sure goods fall off the back of lorries. Straight away, Ross saw that Garner had access to a small goldmine.

The two went into partnership. Ross encouraged Garner to make duplicates of keys to shops being fitted out by the family firm. The pair went back later and robbed them. Ross already had minor convictions and Garner picked up two, in 1958 and 1964, thanks to the City of London police, for handling meat stolen from Smithfield market. But neither of them lingered long in the league of petty criminals. Armed robbery was the new and profitable crime and they studied their profession with care.

The robberies were picked after much planning. In 1972 Garner led his team at high speed up the stairs of the City offices of the bankers Brown Shipley. With him were Kenny Ross, Lennie Gibson, Mickey Sewell, Lennie Minchington — later to be jailed for 20 years for leading the £8 million Bank of America robbery — and a new recruit, Billy Young. They burst into the room where foreign currency was counted and scooped up armfuls. Young recalled later, 'Roy went off and changed it into English money. When he shared it out he told us we had only taken £7,000.' In fact they had stolen £72,000. Garner was learning early how to betray his associates.

The next year Garner 'stuck up' another piece of work, this time at Stratford station in East London. The target was a payroll and he and Ross provided the inside information and a getaway car. Billy Young and two other men grabbed the money. The haul was low, a disappointing £3,000.

The bonus year was 1974. In March, Garner's team tied up

the manager of a London casino and rifled his safe. The big one came later. A security truck carrying nearly £500,000 was waylaid in the South London suburbs. When the money was shared out, there was enough for Garner and Ross to start a new business, a van-hire company in Islington, imaginatively named Kenroys. The bulk of their dealings were with the public but, inevitably, there was a darker side. Vehicles were rented out to fellow criminals for moving stolen goods. It paid well. The company provided the partners with a motor yacht, *Grand Cognac*, and generated the funds to buy property around the corner in Islington's fashionable Upper Street. Year after year the auditors wrestled with the accounts, unable to trace the source of large sums which appeared, as if from nowhere, to buy new vehicles.

More armed robberies were to follow, but Garner was not motivated by the split-second thrill of attack and escape; to him it was business; whatever made money was good. One member of his circle told us, 'Roy Garner's God is a pound note.' That God was served in diverse ways, because Garner was quick to see the possible uses for his increasingly large, disposable income. He became involved in classic 'long firm frauds', where large quantities of goods were obtained on credit from wholesalers. Overnight the business closed down, the proprietors disappeared and the goods were quietly sold on.

The trick nearly came unstuck when Garner bought into a long firm fraud run by his associate Stevie Salter. This time the racket involved wines and spirits. Garner was eager to get the drinks cheaply for a pub he was running. But detectives were watching and, according to Salter, money had to be paid to a detective to smooth things over.

With Ross, Garner put more of their capital into property in London and in the country. They were able to make good deals because most of the time they were inheriting sitting tenants. An arsonist was hired to burn them out and the rebuilding was financed out of insurance policies.

Eventually the van hire business became burdensome and was sold off to relatives of Ross. The proceeds were invested in a finance company and Garner would send gangsters needing capital for criminal enterprises to see the manager. Garner also operated as a loanshark, shaking down people who could not obtain credit elsewhere.

Garner was fast becoming an all-round practitioner of organised crime. He filled the vacuum left by the Kray Twins in North and East London, although in a less ostentatious way. Violence was used sparingly, but when he lost his temper a .22 rifle was at hand for the occasional knee-capping. Other offenders against Garner's interests might be tortured. A beating and some random burning with cigarette ends was usually enough to persuade. It certainly worked on the chest of one woman victim who crossed him.

When Garner and Ross were not out and about with their shotguns they concentrated their efforts on businesses which were cash-rich and could be skimmed ahead of the taxman. In the mid-1960s they took over The Horns pub in Shoreditch. It soon became known as a meeting place for criminal 'faces' and for detectives from City Road police station. The Horns was always good for after-hours drinking and, as supergrass statements revealed later, many crimes were planned in the bar. Lorry hijacking was at its peak during those years, and as Garner and Ross bought large quantities of cheap stolen spirits, The Horns made huge profits.

Sometimes those drinks came virtually free. Garner would buy a lorryload of spirits and keep half for himself. He would then persuade a 'mug' to drive the lorry to a supposedly safe lock-up garage. Astonishingly, when the stolen lorry arrived at its destination, the detectives would be lying in wait. In due course he would probably be able to collect a reward for the goods recovered.

In the early 1970s Garner and Ross moved operations to a new pub, The Eagle, immediately backing on to Tottenham police station. Again, like The Horns, it was a den of thieves and detectives. Many years were to pass before officers from Tottenham police station were banned from drinking next door. Detectives who did call in could count on being welcomed by two ex-Flying Squadmen who had retired early from the Met to work for Garner.

Garner himself watched the till and, as he admitted in private, entertained his criminal friends in 'the Guv'nors corner'. For detectives on duty there was a back room where they could drink undisturbed. Maintaining order at The Eagle was Johnny Brixton who, having already served one sentence for manslaughter, was never happier than when he was threatening somebody with his knife. Brixton's perk was to run his own drinking club upstairs, known as JB's.

Like the Krays before them, Garner and Ross set out to make themselves popular members of their community. At The Eagle they put on cabaret and music shows every night. The shows were free, and as well as the usual bill of fading pop groups, they also paid for stars like The Inkspots, Bob Monkhouse, Lulu and the late Eric Morecambe to appear. They enjoyed having their pictures taken with these celebrities — just like the Krays. Many a local worthy was happy to be photographed receiving a charity cheque from Roy.

The connection to Eric Morecambe, then the brightest star of British comedy, came through yet another pub. Morecambe had married Joan, the sister of Alan Bartlett, who kept The Torrington Arms in Finchley. For years that pub was another key North London venue where the armed robbers could rub shoulders with Robbery Squad officers. Everybody was keen to cash in on the comedian's genius. In the middle 1980s Tony Lundy was to claim, 'Eric Morecambe was a good friend of mine.'

In the late 1970s the old Eagle died. It wasn't attracting the more prosperous younger generation. A great deal of money was raised and the scruffy old pub was reincarnated as Elton's Disco. Garner insisted that he had cleared out the criminals, but it was a lie. They regularly came in the front door to drink late while through the back door they carried on the old trade of dealing in parcels of stolen jewellery. The re-opening night was graced by the cream of London's armed robbers and criminal godfathers and, of course, many of their close friends from the ranks of the detectives. Naturally, Tony Lundy was there.

The glitter was tarnished in November 1981 by a bloody brawl between members of a pop group and the Garner muscle. Garner had to change swiftly out of his blood-splattered clothes and order that the blood on the floor and stairs be washed off before the police from next door arrived. It was alleged that coshes, truncheons and a gun were wielded by the bouncers.

Garner invested in more pubs and clubs, appreciative of the cash flow which could be denied to the taxman. His favourite was the Circle Club in Palmers Green, where his mistresses could be employed as barmaids and private discussions could be held about drug smuggling and distribution.

The two affluent criminals created private lifestyles to match their untaxed riches. Ross bought himself a new neo-Georgian house in Minchenden Crescent, Southgate, and stuffed the driveway with a Porsche, a Mercedes, a BMW and a speedboat.

Around the corner on Cannon Hill, Garner bought the even more grandiose Cannon Lodge and, to comfort his wife June during his many absences, installed a swimming pool and closed-circuit TV cameras to keep criminals at bay. His Rolls-Royce and Mercedes stood out among the cluster of smaller cars for his family.

There was still money left over to invest and it was taken out of the city to the country. In 1968 Garner purchased Holborn Stud Farm, seven acres at Wormley West End near Hertford, and over the years built up his holding to more than 200 acres of pastureland. In the late 1970s Garner finally made the national media when he agreed to stage a bare-knuckle fight between Donny 'The Bull' Adams and Roy 'The Mauler' Shaw at Holborn Farm. Thousands of £5 tickets were sold and, to stop the carnage, the magistrates had to bind over both fighters to keep the peace.

From his uncle Johnny, Garner inherited a fascination for harness racing, where thoroughbred horses trot at high speed towing a lightweight cart and jockey. Lord Langford, President of the British Harness Racing Club, remembers that in his younger days, in the mid-1960s, Garner was a respected jockey. But the noble lord was discomforted by Garner's choice of young female companions, apparently neither daughters nor secretaries, when he visited Langford's North Wales home.

Even though trotting is a minority sport in Britain, Garner poured money into breeding and was soon employing three full-time stable staff. He travelled Europe and North America to buy and sell stock and attended the Toronto horse sales with one of his young mistresses. While he was there, Garner quietly opened a Canadian bank account.

Sport it may have been but Garner could see there was also money to be made. Nine of his horses were kept at a stud in Maryland and more at the Pompano Park track in Fort Lauderdale. It is customary at Pompano for the winning owner to be photographed with his horse and friends at the end of the race. When his thoroughbred 'Pick Me Freely' won on a warm Florida night in 1982 Roy puffed out his chest for the camera, then realised that his blonde mistress was in range. Quickly he thrust her behind the horse — where her legs were captured on film for ever.

Garner's involvement in trotting led him into what should have been his biggest business deal in Britain. He had progressed from millionaire to multi-millionaire and in 1982 used his small change to purchase 105 acres of land, at a cost of £168,500, at Brookmans Park just north of London. Plans were drawn up for a national trotting centre complete with grandstand. He tried to involve Lord Langford, and also Lord Trenchard, who owned land adjoining the proposed track. The key proposal was to have on-course Tote betting. It would have been the nearest racetrack to London and would place Garner squarely on the ground floor of a major new British gambling industry. He had planned to stay in the background but, when his involvement was publicised, the scheme collapsed.

Back in Wormley, Garner built a quarter-mile race track, a luxurious stable block and a £25,000 remedial swimming pool for his horses. Planning permission was granted for a tasteless but spacious ranch-style bungalow. This estate, worth in excess of £500,000, was put out of the reach of any future criminal bankruptcy order. The property was registered in the name of his father, David, who had never earned a penny more than his market porter's wage. However, when Garner wanted to borrow money, he told one of his banks that he was the owner of the estate and that the bungalow had cost £100,000 to build.

Together with Ross he also purchased a nearby livery stables called Tudor Farm. They rented the stables to tenants until it became inconvenient. Then arson and intimidation were employed to drive them out. The police seemed incapable of catching whoever was behind the terror tactics. At weekends Garner entertained local worthies at Holborn Stud and kept in training for his less public profession of armed robbery by shooting over his land with his own legally held shotguns and rifles.

Garner was as greedy in his private life as in his world of crime. His son Mark was born in 1963 and, perhaps because an earlier child had been still-born, was cosseted by both parents. But one family was not enough for Garner. Phyllis Warren, born in Romford just four days before Roy, assumed equal importance in his life. She was a 'hostess' at the notorious Astor Club and in September 1971 gave birth to Roy's daughter. Phyllis was six months pregnant when the couple, calling themselves 'Mr and Mrs Warren', opened an account at Barclays, armed with a false reference which claimed that for 15 years they had been 'most reliable and trustworthy'.

From then on they played games with the bank. Deeds for properties were deposited as security for loans and Garner told the bank he earned £50,000 a year. When it suited them they delayed repaying their loans but Barclays never confronted them. They referred to the 'Warrens' as 'these excellent customers' and recorded on one occasion that they must 'avoid embarrassment to these wealthy customers' and on another that they would 'avoid possible offence to this exceptionally reliable and wealthy customer'.

Garner managed to negotiate such keen rates of interest that eventually Barclays' head office became concerned at the loss of profit. But the 'Warrens' were so pleased with Barclays' service that Phyllis wrote to the bank to introduce a new account, that of her 'nephew' Tony Burrows. In reality this was a false name for Mark Garner.

Roy's first part-time home with Phyllis was in Talbot Road, Highgate, which they bought in 1968. In the 1970s they moved to West Hill Park in the centre of exclusive Old Highgate to be near Hampstead Heath and their daughter's expensive private school. When the house was sold for nearly £200,000 the money was moved offshore to a Canadian bank.

Their property acquisitions rolled on and in the early 1980s, 'Roy and Linda Fisher' spent £160,000 on a Tudor-style detached house in Edmunds Walk, Hampstead. Garner's solicitor, Harold Margolis, held these property documents in his office, marked 'should not be disclosed to June'. Garner was an accomplished liar with his women. He did not tell June, or Phyllis, that he had bought a new apartment in Cedar Grange, Enfield, especially for his blonde mistress. The only link between his homes was that they were all furnished by Harrods. Eventually Phyllis changed her name by deed poll to Garner and Roy rewarded her with a holiday in Florida, prudently checking first that neither his wife nor any of his mistresses would be there at the same time.

There was another private world in which Garner operated. It was a man's world. Garner took his son Mark to Finchley

Amateur Boxing Club, where he was trained by the then Detective Sergeant Tony Lundy. One of the committee members was Lundy's close friend, bookmaker David Spicer. In March 1981 Spicer was arrested by Number 5 Regional Crime Squad, based outside the Metropolitan Police area at Hatfield. They asked him who else was on the committee.

He recalled Ted Williams, whose relatives included a number of gunmen; Lundy's father-in-law, Charlie Moore, and another of Lundy's associates — the millionaire scrap metal dealer and demolition contractor Les Jones. Lundy admits, 'Les Jones is a very close friend of mine.' So close that in 1980 they holidayed together in a Las Vegas hotel. The trip caused concern at Scotland Yard when it was discovered that at the same time a Mob enforcer from the same Vegas hotel was in London seeking the help of one of Lundy's colleagues to collect a bad debt.

When the circus of criminals, the detectives and their businessman friends was not at the boxing club it might be found in Roy Garner's Eagle in Tottenham, at Alan Bartlett's Torrington Arms in Finchley or at The Cavalier at Southgate. During his police interrogation David Spicer recalled gunmen Billy Young and Lennie Gibson drinking at The Cavalier, and also an intriguing list of police officers. 'Jimmy Crane, Ron Page, "Nipper" Read, Reg Lasham, Roy Yorke, Jim Marshall. We come up to date with Tony Lundy, Alec Edwards when he was at Finchley.'

And everywhere was Roy Garner. He had two further occupations which he preferred to keep quiet about. He was the biggest buyer of stolen property in London, the 'fence' that most big-time jewel thieves went to first. They knew he was rich enough to raise £1 million at a few days' notice; he could pay cash for the biggest parcel of stolen gems that might come on the market. Thus Garner was permanently well-informed about who was robbing whom. That led, inexorably, to his other occupation: The Informer.

A regular flow of information from the criminal world went into the Yard's intelligence files under Garner's code-name, 'Dave Granger'. In a secret meeting with a deputy assistant commissioner in 1986 Garner gave his own quaint version of how the skilled detective Lundy had drawn him into becoming a 'grass'. Casting his mind back many years Garner recalled, 'When I see something I didn't like, it started off being told and mentioned, and then he [Lundy] went to that college of yours and learned how to interrogate me without knowing and he drew me out and once you're in, you put your big toe in and you're in, aren't you.'

Rejecting suggestions that Lundy was deeply corrupt, Garner continued, 'They thought they had Lundy as a crooked cozzer working with me. Now that couldn't possibly come to fruition 'cos it wasn't true and Lundy would've sued the pants off everybody. Lundy is not crooked, now I look you in the eye and say that as many times as you need me to say it.'

Garner's version of how Lundy turned him into an informant is as hilarious as his later denials that he conspired to import £100 million-worth of cocaine into Britain. Before he met Lundy, Garner had been an informant for Detective Chief Inspector Alec Eist. The mortician has freed us to write more extensively about Eist, a former member of the Wembley Robbery Squad. He retired hastily from the Yard in the late 1970s having earned more in his career from crime than most of the full-time criminals with whom he consorted.

It was the view of many of his colleagues, and the criminals he pursued with the alacrity of a starving debt collector, that Eist had long lost contact with any normal conception of honesty. His preoccupation was reading the daily crime reports so that he could then hound likely culprits with demands for money.

His favourite stamping ground was Hatton Garden, either setting up robberies or seeking to earn from the frequent ambushes, burglaries and frauds. There he would meet Garner, on his way to sell parcels of precious stones to dealers. In his sharp suits, sunglasses and Mercedes car, Eist played up to his nickname, 'The Godfather'. After his retirement Eist appeared in court in 1979 charged with corruption but was acquitted.

Garner had also talked to a detective chief superintendent. When he retired in the late 1970s to run a pub, Garner concentrated all his attention on his dealings with Tony Lundy. In November 1978 Lundy filed a secret report to his boss, Deputy Assistant Commissioner David Powis, claiming that Garner had been a constant source of information for a number of years and requesting a reward for him.

Rewards of £1,500, £4,000 and £37,500 followed for information allegedly given by Garner about robberies. In 1981

Garner turned his attention to the notorious Barry Brothers, old associates of the Kray Twins. They approached him for a loan. They were busy forging £2 million worth of £5 notes at a secluded factory in Hackney and were short of money to buy a vital piece of equipment. Garner advanced them £3,000 and told Lundy. The Barry Brothers were captured and the next year he was paid a reward.

Garner took the path of his fellow professional criminals in London and began distributing cocaine. But he applied his usual business twist: before completing payment for his consignment he gave information to Lundy. In a private letter to Deputy Assistant Commissioner Powis, Lundy revealed that Garner had told him about 'professional gangsters in England and America . . . one participant is known to have killed an accomplice in connection with another million-pound drug case.'

It would be quite wrong to assume that the now powerful crime boss completely escaped the attentions of the detectives. In the mid-1970s a team from the Met's own Regional Crime Squad, based at West Hendon, decided to target well-known armed robbers and buyers of stolen property. Garner neatly fitted into both categories and the watchers went into place. To their chagrin they found that the moment they started their surveillance Garner seemed, temporarily, to turn his back on crime. Instead he put his efforts into organising boxing meetings at the Royal Lancaster Hotel, which were well attended by detectives from the Robbery Squad.

The detectives who did want to catch Garner may not have known that early in his criminal career he had secured an important line of defence. Together with many of his criminal and detective friends Garner had joined the Freemasons. We may never know if his Freemason detective friends protected him from investigation and prosecution, although there is evidence of other masonic criminals working in league with Met masonic detectives. In Garner's case there is only one clear piece of evidence. He attended the meetings of the Bishop Ridley Lodge held at the Great Eastern Hotel, close by Liverpool Street station, and a Met detective sergeant member of the lodge helped him buy shotguns and obtain a gun licence. The irony would not have been lost on the armed robber.

3 · THE FIRM

SCOTLAND YARD'S TOP DETECTIVE was born in a modest house, in the hamlet of New Springs, deep in the Lancashire mining belt near Wigan. At weekends Tony Lundy would climb nearby Rivington Pike and gaze south towards Manchester, Liverpool and the rich Cheshire plain. But his sights were set further afield.

Lundy came from a humble Catholic family. His father, John, was a bricklayer's labourer and also, at the time of his son's birth in April 1942, a watcher in the National Fire Service. Fifteen months later, and 200 miles away, Violet Moore was born in Hackney in London's East End. Her father Charlie was from an equally lowly background. In peacetime he was a hide merchant's clerk but the war had taken him away to be an able seaman in the Royal Navy.

Tony and Violet married in May 1966 at St Ignatius Church on Tottenham High Road, midway between Roy Garner's old pub, The Horns, and The Eagle, to which he would soon move. Violet was a bank clerk and Tony, who had come to London to join the Metropolitan Police in 1962, had just become a Detective Constable.

The young Lundy had done well. He was quick-witted and had profited from his early postings. First he was sent to Islington and Kings Cross, where he walked the beat in the tough inner-city crime villages. Gentrification was creeping into Islington but, for all the hyperbole in the estate agents' brochures, it was and is still the home of some of the capital's most senior robbers. After three years learning his trade he moved to the adjacent Hackney division which included City Road police station and its nearby pub – The Horns.

Lundy's experience was increasing fast. A year later he moved on to yet another area with rich pickings for determined detectives. 'E' District runs from Holborn up into Camden and includes Albany Street police station. Now he was operating on the edge of the West End with its clubs, vice and porn rackets.

It was not easy to support a family on a constable's wages. Police pay lagged behind in the 'never had it so good' 60s while the villains prospered. Lundy's first daughter was born in 1967 and was followed in the next three years by two sisters. Despite the poor wages the Lundys struggled to give their daughters expensive private schooling.

Lundy's ambition was recognised by his superiors and his next posting took him northwards to the area where, in the years to come, he would make his name. In 1968 he was promoted to second-class sergeant and his territory covered Barnet, Finchley and Golders Green. Despite being outside the city centre it was an area where many robbers lived, socialised and sometimes carried out their bank raids.

Now Lundy made two of the friendships that would last throughout the rest of his police career. At the bookmaker's in Ballards Lane, Finchley, he met David Spicer, and at The Torrington Arms he joined landlord Alan Bartlett's clientele, partly made up of gunmen and detectives. He was also keen to become accepted at the Finchley Boxing Club by committee members like Ted Williams and Les Jones.

Roy Garner, Kenny Ross, Lennie Gibson and the rest of their gangster circuit were always at hand to share in fund raising for the club. Although Lundy, as a Catholic, did not join the Freemasons, many of his new friends, detectives, gunmen and businessmen, were 'on the square'.

To be near his new friends, Lundy and his family moved to Borehamwood on the green edge of London. The career break he had been praying for came in December 1969 when he was accepted into the Flying Squad, with its freedom to course across the whole metropolis. He spent time at West End Central police station and learned about the sharks of Soho. The bad habits of some of the old-style Soho detectives rubbed off and Lundy was unwise enough to be photographed at a swish function in a West End hotel in the company of Garner, Ross and gunman Lennie Gibson. In a second picture he was completely obscured in the back row but, unfortunately, his profile and distinctive sideburns were captured in a mirror at one side of the group. Lundy was to make few such mistakes again. Far too many detectives had dubious relationships with criminals but the endemic corruption in some areas of the Met CID was concealed from the outside world. Eventually the dam burst and Lundy's rise in the CID would take place during massive upheavals at New Scotland Yard.

In the golden age of the Flying Squad the senior officers were household names. On their retirement, these legendary men would publish memoirs of their dozen best cases, and one in this 'Jorrocks of the Yard' genre came from Detective Chief Superintendent Jack Slipper in the early 1980s.

He thought corruption so negligible that he did not mention any of the notorious cases of his era. Some of his contemporaries have different memories. Slipper was one of the many Squadmen who worked on the investigation into the 1962 Great Train Robbery, when £2.6 million was stolen from a mail train. It has since been the subject of numerous films and books and is still talked about as the 'crime of the century'. Many, but not all of the robbers were caught, and considerable sums of money recovered, most of which was returned to the owners.

There was one area of the investigation which did not in any way involve Slipper and it puzzled him. 'There was another recovery of cash that we never did find an explanation for . . . an anonymous phone tip came in telling us to go and look in a telephone box in Southwark.'

The detectives did look and found £48,000 in a sack. The money had been left there after delicate negotiations between one of the robbers and certain detectives. By this stage the majority of the robbers had been caught and the image of the Squad was high. Now it was time to do some business. Twenty-six years after the Great Train Robbery the man who left the money there, and who had had a key role in the robbery, told us what had happened.

'When we cut the money up each of us got a whack of £150,000. Sure it was a lot of money but we had expected twice as much on the train, as much as £5 million. I left my share with people I could trust and was warned that it would be wise to leave town for a while. In all I was away for about nine months. Word was passed to me that the police knew I had been on the robbery, but there was no forensic evidence to tie me in. I had been careful.

'The deal was quite straightforward. I had to pay money to the police and I had to give a big lump of it back so they would look as if they were doing well. It was arranged that about £50,000 would be left in a phone box for them to find. And there was some more for them. Funnily enough, they didn't ask for a lot. It was about £2,000. That's all. Then I had to go in and be interviewed and cleared of suspicion. Mind you, when I went in to see the police, I couldn't be sure that they wouldn't go crooked on me. And in fact, when I got there, one of the policemen wanted to go crooked on the deal, even after he had had the money. But there were only two of them involved and he was talked out of it. I walked out free with the guarantee that although they knew I had been on the train, they had had their money and I wouldn't be fitted up. That was what I needed.

'Corruption? Back in the 50s and 60s it was rampant. It seemed as if they all were. You paid money all the time. Yet the demands varied. Back in the 1950s I paid a detective £100 not to tell the court what my previous convictions were. Just £100 to say "Nothing known, Sir." It was worth a lot more to me.'

That robber still lives in London, and he agreed to talk only after long negotiations and an understanding that we would never identify him. His story, well-known in London police and criminal circles, would not have been believed at the time.

All that changed on the morning of Saturday 29 November 1969, one month before Lundy was promoted to the Flying Squad. *The Times* led its front page with stark allegations that London detectives took bribes from criminals and offered favours in return. The Yard could not shrug the story off because the reporters had captured its key evidence on tape.

One of those tapes recorded a detective giving fatherly advice to a young thief. 'Don't forget to let me know straight away if you need anything because I know people everywhere. Because I'm in a little firm in a firm. Don't matter where, anywhere in

London I can get on the phone to someone I know I can trust, that talks the same as me. And if he's not the right person that can do it, he'll know the person that can. All right? That's the thing and it can work well, it's worked well for years, hasn't it . . . we've got more villains in our game than you have got in yours, you know.'

The image of a 'Firm within a Firm' has dogged the Yard ever since, despite the hierarchy moving swiftly to limit the damage. *The Times* story claimed that 'at least three detectives are taking large sums of money in exchange for dropping charges, for being lenient with evidence offered in court and for allowing a criminal to work unhindered. Our investigations into the activities of these three men convince us that this case is not isolated. We cannot prove that the other officers are guilty but we believe that there is enough suspicion to justify a full inquiry.'

In the hours before going to press *The Times* had dutifully passed over its evidence to the Met. Several days were allowed to elapse before the homes, desks and lockers of the three officers were searched. No move was made to suspend them at an early stage of the inquiry and the three corrupt detectives started to nobble potential witnesses.

Detective Chief Superintendent Bill Moody was appointed to lead the internal investigation. It would be another seven years before the world discovered what a catastrophic move this was. Insiders at the Yard knew that the inquiry could have led to the successful prosecution of as many as twenty-five detectives but, strangely, the efforts of top detective Moody made no progress.

It was one of the Met's finer damage limitation exercises in a long history of successful cover-ups, and it triumphed over the press, Parliament and also the efforts of a dedicated opponent of corruption brought in to try and keep the inquiry on an honest footing. Frank Williamson, HM Inspector of Constabulary for the North West, former chief constable son of a chief constable was given an advisory brief by the Home Office, the first outsider ever allowed to investigate crime within the Met.

Eventually he resigned in disgust because of the gross obstruction he encountered. Two detectives were jailed eventually for six and seven years, branded as the occasional rotten apples that any force might discover within its ranks, and the Met breathed again. The third left the country before his trial, and when he returned in 1980 he was jailed for 18 months. On his release he made serious allegations against a number of senior officers, whom he claimed had been corrupt alongside him in the junior ranks a decade earlier.

The groundwork that made the public believe corruption allegations was laid by the Met itself. During the 1960s the young middle classes, who thought the police dealt solely with a lower strata of society, suddenly found themselves on the sharp end of the Drugs Squad. Members of the underground rather than the underworld, they were astonished to find that some detectives would casually plant drugs on them or extort bribes not to prosecute them.

Anyone who ventured into dealing soon discovered that Drugs Squad officers might happily steal a large proportion of the illicit substances and then bring charges of possessing small amounts for personal consumption. It was a state of affairs that suited both parties but opened the eyes of the educated classes to police practices that had been perfected over the decades.

In May 1969 Victor Kelaher was appointed head of the Drugs Squad. He had learned his trade in two spells on the Flying Squad and was the youngest Detective Chief Inspector in the Yard's history. In the three years that he ran the Squad it became famous in London's hippy world for the curious kind of deals that could be negotiated. Drugs seized in busts were either sold back to the dealers they had been taken from or given to other dealers who were also informants. Some informants were allowed to deal drugs relatively unhindered as long as they delivered 'bodies' for conviction.

The dubious activities of Kelaher's team became the subject of a *World in Action* investigation and simultaneously the Home Office received disturbing reports from provincial detectives who had come in contact with the Squad. However, the Yard hierarchy resisted interference and guaranteed Kelaher protection against his critics even after the day when Customs and Excise drugs investigators detained him during a West London swoop on cannabis importers.

Customs (part of the Treasury) had been tapping the smugglers' phones and knew that Kelaher was very close to the importation; Kelaher's bosses (answerable to the Home Office) saw no reason to suspend or discipline him. In July 1970 the Yard was forced to accept another outside inquiry, this time by Harold Prescott, Chief Constable of Lancashire. Yet more public money had to be spent because of the Yard's inability to police itself. It was hardly surprising that Prescott suffered as much obstruction as Frank Williamson before him. The insular senior ranks at the Yard shrugged off the poor publicity this saga brought. They knew they had won again.

Kelaher and several of his officers were eventually charged with conspiracy. Two detective sergeants and a detective constable were jailed for perjury but Kelaher was acquitted. In April 1974 he was allowed to retire on a medical pension, ahead of what a Minister of State told Parliament would have been 'serious allegations at disciplinary proceedings'.

A frequent guest at some of the Yard's social functions in the early 1970s was an expert in organised crime, vice, racketeering and gang warfare. His every need was seen to and he was among friends. To show his gratitude for such treatment he and his colleagues ensured that many of the detectives were paid hundreds of thousands of pounds, supplied with holidays, cars, jewellery and the services of his 'models'.

In 1974, an elite Yard team, the Serious Crime Squad, had that special guest, Bernie Silver, jailed for his services to pornography and the Soho sex trade. The Squad was led by Albert 'The Old Grey Fox' Wickstead and his detectives succeeded because they kept much of their investigations secret from their colleagues. Silver's six-year sentence was to be the curtain-raiser to a succession of corruption trials that brought the reputation of the Yard to its lowest ebb.

Corrupt detectives had always earned from the clubs in Soho, running protection rackets with which the gangsters could never compete. The explosion in payments came in the 1960s with the increasing demand for illegal pornography. Silver swiftly organised the majority of the Soho dirty bookshops and then did the same with the detectives entrusted to stop him.

His monopoly ran for nearly a decade. But conflict loomed in 1969 when Soho clubowner Jimmy Humphreys decided to set up his own porn shops. Humphreys sought advice from his friend Commander Wallace Virgo, who sponsored a meeting with both Silver and the officer in charge of the Obscene Publications Squad, Detective Chief Superintendent Bill Moody. With far more energy than he was ever to invest in the inquiries following

The Times disclosures, Moody began to organise one of the most horrifyingly corrupt episodes in the history of the Met.

The pornographers were encouraged to expand their businesses and the detectives protected them and warned off any competition. Virgo was one of the Yard's premier detectives and already had national responsibility for prison security following a series of dramatic escapes. As the courts were to hear later, a team of detectives under Virgo and Moody gleefully accepted monstrous rewards from the pornographers.

Senior ranks at the Yard appeared to be indifferent to the crooks in their midst, and it was left to the press to force the rackets into the open. In August 1971 the *Observer* published a long investigation into the porn business which was followed six months later by two onslaughts from the *People*. The paper struck hard. It named a number of the biggest porn operators, then revealed that Jimmy Humphreys had just returned from holidaying in Cyprus with Commander Ken Drury, head of the Flying Squad. Drury was instantly suspended and soon left the force.

Bert Wickstead was given the job of breaking open the swindles. He targeted Humphreys and had him jailed for eight years for slashing his wife's lover to ribbons. Eager to trade his way out of jail, Humphreys revealed that he had kept diaries of his corrupt dealings! The pornographer made lengthy statements to Commander Ron Steventon, naming 38 detectives.

The list grew as other pornographers, feeling the new chill wind, decided to co-operate. One named a staggering 148 officers; another estimated that up to £250,000 a year had been bled from him by corrupt policemen. The individual stories of buying protection, warning of raids, and of buying back seized material from police station vaults appalled the Yard's keenest apologists. It also emerged that many of the leading pornographers and their bent police friends belonged to the same Masonic lodges.

Humphreys provided new pointers to how the Yard protected its own in-house criminals. He had made a formal complaint to the Yard about being shaken down for money by Detective Sergeant Harry Challenor. The Yard replied: 'The Commissioner is satisfied that the officer has acted perfectly correctly.' When Challenor was later caught planting half-bricks on demonstrators against Queen Frederika and the Greek fascist junta he had to be charged, but the protection continued. Challenor was suddenly declared mad and removed beyond the reach of justice to psychiatric care. 'The Firm' was saved but the number of people becoming sceptical about Scotland Yard was growing.

The only encouraging aspect of the three porn trials that followed was that junior officers gave evidence for the prosecution. Several had been forced to make payments to senior officers to get transferred away from the stench of policing Soho. In all, 13 detectives were jailed for a total of 98 years, Moody and Virgo both going away for 12 years, although Virgo subsequently had his conviction quashed. Drury was sentenced to eight years, reduced by the Appeal Court to five, which in reality became 26 months, mainly in Ford open prison in Sussex.

The Yard's mishandling of the inquiries into *The Times* allegations, coupled with the drugs and pornography scandals, guaranteed that when the Commissioner's chair next became vacant it would not be offered to any time-served Met man. Robert Mark was already Deputy Commissioner, having been drafted in from provincial service in Manchester and then Leicester. He was an outsider and the CID made it clear that he was unwelcome. The more these senior officers resisted his demands for reform, the more certain it was that he would be appointed to the top job when it fell vacant in early 1972.

Few critics of the Yard have penned more severe strictures than Mark in his autobiography, *In the Office of Constable*. He was a defender of decent policemen but appalled at the pettiness of many of his subordinates, of whom he wrote, 'the imagination boggles at the intellectual capacity and inhumanity'. When he took over responsibility for internal investigations he was horrified by the free-ranging corruption and indiscipline of the CID, who existed as a virtually independent force within the force.

He wrote: 'I had never experienced institutionalised wrongdoing, blindness, arrogance and prejudice on anything like the scale accepted as routine in the Met.' His initial efforts to bring the CID under control won immediate support from uniform officers 'who were only too pleased to see someone deal with a department which had long brought the force as a whole into disgrace'. During the next four years Mark forced the resignations of hundreds of officers despite the opposition of the CID.

The grossness of the CID's determination to protect its own deviants, compared with its enthusiasm for investigating and punishing the uniform men, provided the foundations on which the politician Mark built cleverly. The isolation of the CID ended when all 2,300 detectives not on elite squads were placed under the supervision of their divisional uniformed commanders, whose responsibilities included discipline and promotion. At a stroke the bonds of loyalty up and down the CID ladder were broken. Regular interchange between uniform and CID was introduced and detectives who resisted postings to uniform found their promotion hopes dashed.

The other crucial innovation was the creation of the A10 department. From that moment the power to investigate allegations of disciplinary and criminal behaviour was wrenched for ever from the bosom of the CID and vested in this new department within the uniform section of the Yard.

Mark commented, optimistically, 'Even the dumbest detective must have understood that if he was obstructive his days in the CID were numbered.' But some *were* so dumb — or confident that they could survive the purges. The new Commissioner discovered that his measures were 'bitterly opposed by some detectives and their journalistic associates. Every kind of device was tried to mislead and alarm the public and diminish their acceptability.'

Mark's response was uncompromising: he confronted the CID and told them bluntly that they represented 'what had long been the most routinely corrupt organisation in London'. They were warned that if change did not come quickly he would put them all back in uniform and rebuild his detective branch afresh. Later Mark noted that after the setting up of A10 'the arrest of detectives attempting routine extortion and blackmail rose sharply'. It must be granted to Robert Mark that his changes did bring long overdue fresh air. He made virtue fashionable.

4 · SUPERGRASS

THE CORRUPT DETECTIVES were so occupied collecting their Soho bribes, and their share of the swelling drugs trade, that they failed, literally, to hear the sound of gunfire on the horizon. By the early 1970s the armed robbers were working the streets of London with impunity, assaulting banks, security trucks and Hatton Garden jewellers, seemingly at will.

As ever, the Yard had an explanation for its failure to stop this banditry. Apparently these robberies were the work of the 'mysteries', scores of as yet unknown but clever criminals living anonymously in the suburbs who banded together for one-off jobs. The Yard conveyed the impression of baffled detectives scratching their heads in confusion about how on earth to identify these new 'super crooks'. Roy Garner and Lennie Gibson and the other members of the North London Circus would have found this picture amusing if they had ever had time to step back from the business of getting seriously, criminally, rich.

The truth was that the majority of dedicated detectives had a very good idea who the villains were. They had been tracking them from their earliest days in petty crime up to their joining the top league of gunmen. The detectives were getting good criminal intelligence from their informants and they acted on it, frequently recommending the arrest of suspects. Too often they would stand by powerless as the robbers were brought into police stations, interviewed by certain detectives, not asked to give full account of their movements or the usual forensic samples of hair, blood and saliva for matching against evidence found at scenes of crime and then put back on the streets. Within days the informants would bring news of how much had been paid for these 'soft' interviews which virtually guaranteed that the robbers would not be troubled again by the attentions of the police. In effect, many armed robbers had bought themselves licences to terrorise the public.

The bent detectives not only wanted a share of the haul from recent robberies, they sometimes sought payment in advance. One well-known robber of the time told us how troublesome this could be. 'On a Thursday and Friday you couldn't even go out three-handed in a car near City Road nick without being stopped and a detective taking a few hundred quid off you.' A refusal to hand over money, the robber explained, could result in being arrested and 'verballed'. Detectives would concoct a confession of conspiracy to rob, and to help it stick, shotguns would be planted in the boots of their cars.

The Yard desperately sought to stem the soaring crime statistics. Instead of seeking out obvious corruption within the Met, the top bosses preferred to throw money and manpower on to the streets. The plan failed. The robbers were not deterred.

Finally the Yard came up with an answer. It turned the whole rationale of detective work on its head. Instead of a remorseless campaign to capture and convict the criminals, the Yard, backed by the legal establishment, conceded defeat. They resurrected the centuries-old technique of encouraging thieves to turn 'Queen's Evidence' and testify against their comrades in return for leniency. The policy did put many of the robbers in prison; it also guaranteed freedom to some of the worst offenders.

The phenomenon, quickly dubbed the 'supergrass' system by the tabloids, flourished for a decade and the public was diverted by the sight of hundreds of robbers being jailed for thousands of years — and a drop in the robbery statistics. In its early stages the supergrass policy brought much good publicity to the Yard, a point that could not have been lost on the ambitious Tony Lundy. The policy also made one violent gunman famous, free and rich.

Bertie Smalls was a professional armed robber in London for the best part of a decade without being unduly troubled by the police. In his own words he was 'a pretty good frightener' and even today, as he drinks in North and West London pubs, no hard man is keen to punish him for becoming a 'grass'. Bertie, it is said, can still handle himself.

On 10 August 1972 that was all too evident to the terrified staff and customers at Barclays Bank in Wembley High Road, when a team of six masked men, led by Smalls, burst through the doors, fired a shot into the ceiling to show they meant business and departed 90 seconds later with £138,000 in used notes. The Met's manner of solving the crime sent shock waves through London's armed robbers.

Within days an informant disclosed the names of two of the robbers, Bruce Brown and Bryan Turner. The names of more suspects were suggested. Danny Allpress, who had been on the robbery, was taken in for interview but, inexplicably, allowed to leave. A further suspect, Phil Morris, was brought in for questioning and also released. Two months later he shot a man dead during an armed robbery in Surrey. According to Yard intelligence, Lennie Gibson was one of the robbers although he had nothing to do with the shooting.

Bruce Brown was the first to be charged. He had a key to a safe deposit box which was found to contain some of the stolen Wembley cash. Despite this success results were not coming fast enough, and so the Yard set up a special robbery squad. Chief Superintendent James Marshall and Chief Inspector Alec Eist were sent to Wembley to take charge. As the detectives persevered the name they heard most frequently was that of Bertie Smalls. He had been a robber since the mid-1960s and was no stranger to corrupt detectives. But the pressure was on for results, and finally Smalls was tracked down in the Midlands in Christmas week 1972.

It was soon clear that there was enough evidence to charge him with two robberies, but there was not enough evidence to arrest the remainder of the Wembley team. A deal with Smalls seemed imperative if the Yard was to get the result it so badly needed. After secret negotiations it was agreed that Smalls would make a full confession and name all his associates. The price was complete immunity from all his crimes. The deal even allowed him to keep the proceeds of his robberies which, in a later TV interview, he admitted were in the region of £300,000.

Sir Norman Skelhorn, the Director of Public Prosecutions, approved the deal in April 1973 and Smalls immediately started talking. He confessed to 15 robberies and gave information on seven more. More than 30 associates were named. He appeared in court where 'no evidence' was offered against him. Smalls then spent the remainder of 1973 and 1974 giving evidence against his former friends. Whatever the faults in the Smalls deal, it has to be allowed that a large number of very dangerous robbers were taken out of circulation for a very long time. The only concern must be why they were not captured long before. In court Smalls' fellow robbers did not miss any opportunity to claim that they had been verballed and that detectives had stolen money from them and had also been bribed into 'dropping them out' of earlier inquiries.

The convicted men went to the Appeal Court in March 1975 and two were freed for lack of corroboration, but most of the sentences were confirmed.

Then Lord Chief Justice Lawton exploded, calling Smalls 'a craven villain' and adding, 'Above all else the spectacle of the Director [Sir Norman Skelhorn] recording in writing, at the behest of a criminal like Smalls, his undertaking to give immunity from further prosecution is one which we find distasteful. Nothing of a similar kind must happen again.'

However that was far from the end of the Wembley affair. Even as the press were trumpeting, 'the most successful robbery investigation since the war', allegations were emerging that the old 'Firm within a Firm' was intact and still doing business. What was at stake was the considerable reward money offered by the clearing banks to encourage informants to name the Wembley gunmen.

Three days after Smalls and his team hit Barclays in Wembley, Joan Angell, a detective constable on the Flying Squad, got a call from one of her best informants, a woman code-named 'Mary Frazer'. It was the first breakthrough in the Wembley investigation. Frazer revealed that two of the robbers were Bruce Brown and Bryan Turner.

Their names were passed to Detective Inspector Vic Wilding who, initially, was in charge of the investigation. For the following fortnight Angell watched Turner who, having dispatched his family to Spain, was staying on in London 'to see what the police were up to'. Turner was so well informed about police intentions that he boarded a flight for Spain an hour before detectives raided his empty house.

The day after Brown was charged, Angell told Wilding that she was going to nominate Mary Frazer for a reward. Wilding then disclosed that he had an informant of his own and Frazer had not contributed to Brown's capture. Angell decided to wait until Turner had also been caught before pursuing the reward for Mary Frazer. Eleven months later Turner was extradited from Spain and on 13 August 1973, a year to the day after Mary Frazer had given the crucial names, Angell filed her reward claim.

Frazer was clearly close to the Wembley gang because she had provided a second piece of information within days of Brown's arrest. It cast a cloud over the investigation. Brown's safe deposit box had been taken, unopened, by Detective Inspector Wilding and Detective Chief Superintendent Dick Saxby to Wembley police station. When they emerged hours later from behind a locked door they announced that the box contained nearly £15,000 from the Wembley bank.

Frazer passed on the news that Brown's family was outraged; they claimed there had been about £55,000 in the box when it fell into police hands. Angell raised this allegation at an afternoon conference of the Robbery Squad at Wembley. One officer present remembers, 'There was silence followed by a group of detectives going very red in the face.' Angell was bustled out to a nearby pub by friends who warned her to watch her back. The allegation was raised again at Brown's trial and later in some intriguing, covertly made tape-recordings.

Mary Frazer was becoming impatient for her reward. In December 1973, she wrote to Commissioner Mark complaining, 'I have been taken for a fool.' Chief Superintendent Anthony Platt of the new A10 internal investigations department was appointed to examine her allegations. He soon discovered that Wilding and Saxby had had a busy month after the Wembley robbery. They too, it turned out, had secured the services of an excellent informant. He was code-named 'William Wise'.

The detectives claimed that Wise had told them about Brown's safe deposit box containing the stolen money. For this Wise was paid £350 from the Met's Informants' Fund and another £500 by Barclays Bank. Wilding also claimed that Wise had named a robber involved in a £50,000 armed robbery at a West London post office. The Post Office gave Wilding a further £75 to hand over to Wise. This intrigued Angell as, within a day of that robbery, Mary Frazer had given her the same name and she had logged this information.

Platt's inquiry then discovered that Wilding and Saxby had made a second Wembley robbery reward recommendation for Wise. Apparently Wise had told them that the robber Bryan Turner also had a safe deposit box, and that it contained £11,000 from the Wembley raid. On the strength of this second report Barclays handed out another £500 for Wise and the Met gave him a further £200.

There are many confusions about Wilding and Saxby's story. During the Wembley investigation Commissioner Robert Mark invited a team of journalists from the *Sunday Times* to chronicle the Robbery Squad's success. Their story of Brown's box is at odds with the versions given to A10 by Wilding and Saxby. Detectives interviewed by the journalists recalled that when they were at the vault containing Brown's box they had shown the staff pictures of Turner. They then identified him as the owner of another box. There was not one word said about inside information — just good old fashioned detective work.

Wilding and Saxby had anticipated criticism: they put in a report saying, 'Vile rumours are circulating throughout the underworld regarding the integrity of police officers attached to this squad. Let it be said now that reliable information has been received that these rumours have been deliberately spread to stop further police action in this matter.'

An increasingly angry and suspicious Mary Frazer wrote again to Commissioner Mark. 'I am wondering *if* this money has gone to an informant [our italics].' Frazer was not alone in her suspicions. As the inquiry dragged on a senior officer on the A10 team broke ranks and urged that a 'substantial sum' should be handed over to Frazer as an *ex gratia* payment. He claimed, 'Obstruction is being encountered within the force and an inquiry is being denied all the evidence necessary to prove or disprove the informant's allegations and, for that matter, the guilt or innocence of the various officers involved, some of senior rank.' Shortly after writing this dissenting report he was transferred to divisional work.

The report Platt produced in February 1975 lit more fires than it doused. His summary of Frazer's complaint was that she had given information but not been rewarded. In fact Frazer had made it clear that she did not believe there was another informant at all; she was suggesting a conspiracy by detectives to hijack information and pocket the reward money. Her accusation also carried the implication that there would be attempts to impede the investigation.

This indeed was the case as Platt recorded it. Time and again officers, many of them very senior policemen, simply could not remember who had said what and when. This was also the case when it came to finding records of Angell's report recommending a reward for Frazer. Her report had disappeared from the files and somebody had also deleted the fact that she had submitted it.

Chief Superintendent Platt met Mary Frazer twice at Joan Angell's West London home and took statements from her over tea. His meeting with Wise was more dramatic. The mystery informant was produced at Heathrow airport in a car with darkened windows. He wore sunglasses, his hat was well down and his collar up. Platt was told that Wise frequented West London criminal circles and had a criminal record. Platt said in his report that he suspected Mary Frazer too had criminal convictions. Former detective Joan Angell vigorously refutes this.

Platt summed up that while 'one cannot conclude that it was only Wise's information which brought about this happy event . . . it cannot be said he has been wrongly rewarded or that the actions of the police officers dealing with him have, in any way, been improper. Insofar as the payments to Wise are concerned there is no evidence of impropriety and nothing of a criminal nature has been disclosed.'

Platt allowed that Frazer had been treated 'shabbily' and suggested that there was moral justification in her claim to a share of the rewards. Then he ruled that her complaint was unsubstantiated. This decision left senior officers in the clear, Angell rejected and Frazer unpaid. In January 1974 Angell had a meeting with Commissioner Mark at which she laid out her complaints and told him that she would resign as soon as the Frazer case was resolved. A year later the London clearing banks paid Frazer £1,000, the same sum as

'Wise' had received. The scandal was then raised in the House of Commons by Phillip Whitehead MP, who described Angell as 'a policewoman of impeccable reputation' and called for a public inquiry.

Shortly after Angell left the Met, Wilding followed her out, and became a security officer for Barclays Bank. Three years later Wilding was charged with perverting the course of justice and stealing £3,000 worth of traveller's cheques back in 1971. At that time Wilding had been one of a team of detectives sent to smash the 'Thiefrow' organisation of baggage handlers at Heathrow airport. The Old Bailey was told that, with another detective, Wilding had stolen the cheques and then commissioned a well-known Soho pornographer to launder them. Both men denied the charges, and were acquitted.

There were still more problems which blemished the 'success' with Smalls. The A10 investigation next turned its attention to the allegation that Detective Chief Superintendent Saxby and others had helped themselves to around £40,000 from Bruce Brown's deposit box.

During Brown's trial it had been disclosed that the gunman and detective Saxby were frequent golfing and lunch companions. They and their wives had holidayed together in Germany. Brown had even popped into Wembley police station for coffee with Saxby while junior detectives were out hunting the Barclays robbers. Brown was also invited to the celebrations when Saxby was promoted to Detective Chief Superintendent.

The allegation came from the robber's wife, Mrs Glenys Brown. She had made three remarkable tape-recordings of telephone conversations between herself and her good friend Mrs Eunice Saxby. The detective's wife claimed that soon after Brown's box was opened Saxby had returned home clutching two briefcases full of money. A10 found nothing to concern them in Mrs Brown's allegations. However, Saxby was officially listed as 'sick' and, for reasons the Yard has never disclosed, was required to resign. Questions were asked in the Commons about the nature of Saxby's illness but with his pension and without his wife he emigrated to Miami.

Shortly before leaving Saxby gave an exclusive interview to the *Daily Mail* in which he said there was 'an innocent explanation' for his association with Brown, adding, 'This embarrassing relationship was possible because there was no system for alerting senior officers to the identity of people who became key suspects during investigations.' It was not explained how Saxby, a very senior detective in West London over many years, had remained unaware of Brown's two previous prison sentences.

5 · LUNDY'S FACTORY

SUPERGRASS SMALLS BROUGHT THE MET the success it so desperately needed against the gunmen. Suddenly the detectives were beginning to look effective. But behind closed doors at the Yard the leadership of the CID was in chaos. By 1977 an outside force was investigating serious corruption allegations and, although never substantiated, they led to damaging media stories. Deputy Assistant Commissioner Reg Davies, operational head of the CID, chose to retire rather than be suspended until the conclusion of the inquiry and Jock Wilson OBE, the Assistant Commissioner in charge of Crime, was transferred to the Traffic Department.

Wilson was replaced by Gilbert Kelland, who had led the successful inquiry into the Porn Squad and restored some confidence in the claim that the Yard could investigate its own criminals. Kelland's deputy was David Powis, switched from the Traffic Department. *Police Review* commented blandly, '50-year-old DAC Powis is returning to CID having left the CID last when he was promoted to uniform sergeant in 1956.'

Powis knew little about the contemporary world of detectives and first division robbers. In some ways this was an advantage: he had no personal loyalties or debts to officers who might face allegations. On the other hand, the CID had changed a lot in the 21 years he had been away. Many of the career detectives, straight and bent alike, viewed him at first with amusement and later with disdain.

His appointment was seen as a victory for the uniform section over a CID that still had pockets of corruption. Some CID officers were put out by his formal style, his demand that jackets and ties should be worn in the office, and his preference for being addressed as 'Sir'. Powis's use of language seemed Edwardian, often relied on cricketing metaphor and was worlds apart from the streetwise talk of his detectives.

One senior officer who served under Powis recalls, 'He quickly established that he wished to be known as an eccentric and often wore a three-piece pin-striped suit with a tweed fishing hat, complete with flies, while he stalked the corridors. His language was quaint, using such terms as "gainsay me gentlemen" at conferences.'

Powis soon became known as 'Crazy Horse' by officers who found his judgments erratic. It was a title he enjoyed, believing it implied relentless energy. Powis quickly termed himself 'Head of Detectives' and was soon seen waving captured sawn-offs at press conferences after gunmen had been arrested.

Although Powis was in overall charge of operations and removed from day-to-day detective work, he sought close contacts with informants. The quality of a detective is often measured by the worth of his or her informants — and their ability to operate in this minefield. Powis was to oversee a period when the Yard relied increasingly on informants and supergrasses. Eventually his career became entwined with one of the Yard's most controversial informer episodes.

Less flamboyant and rarely interviewed by the media was Powis's equal, DAC Ron Steventon, who was in charge of CID administration. Many felt that the real brains of the CID was the shrewder, and far more experienced, Steventon.

When the newly appointed Commissioner, David McNee, sat down with Powis and their new colleagues and looked at the ever increasing crime figures it was clear the public was not being well served. Burglary, mugging, auto-thefts and rape were soaring and, despite the passing success with Bertie Smalls, armed robbery was flourishing again. There had been 27 bank robberies in 1976. By the middle of 1977 the total was already 28.

The hard-pressed ratepayers of London might have hoped that the new men at the Yard would crack down on the street crime that plagued their lives. After all, armed robbery amounted to no more than 2 per cent of London lawlessness. But the new leadership fell in line with the traditional thinking of the CID elite: the destruction of the classic enemy, the hard core of cash-laden armed robbers, had to come first.

The Flying Squad was reorganised in mid-1978 and the majority of the detectives were redeployed into a new 'Robbery Squad' with four units spread around the capital. Within months one team was making the headlines. It was the North London Robbery Squad, it was based at Finchley and it was led by Tony Lundy.

In 1973 he had been made an inspector and at the end of the year his abilities were recognised and rewarded by a two-year posting to the Detective Training School at Hendon. One of the detectives who was later to investigate corruption allegations against him recalled, 'Unlike some cops Lundy didn't lose contact with the streets. When he wasn't at Hendon he was out and about, keeping up with the criminal intelligence.' Lundy kept in touch with his friends in the North London Circus and was seen frequently at charity functions organised by Finchley Boxing Club.

The Lundy family was also on the move again, to a pleasant house in Cowley Hill Road, Borehamwood. The property was graced by an expensive new timber fence, which was delivered one Saturday morning. At the end of his stint at Hendon, Tony Lundy was transferred to Wembley, and 18 months later he was ready when the call came. In May 1977 the newly promoted Detective Chief Inspector Lundy was rotated back into the Flying Squad and sent off to Finchley.

By 1980 his name was a word reviled in the capital's criminal circles. It was quick work; one of London's leading armed robbers from the 1960s onwards, told us over a half-pint, 'We never heard of Lundy before the mid-70s.'

In the space of three years Tony Lundy became the star detective at Scotland Yard. His declarations from the Old Bailey witness box of 'a war against crime' were headlined by the press and the Yard put him forward on TV as their ace thief-taker. At one trial after another he saw armed robbers given long jail sentences and then went off to relax with Roy Garner at the Torrington pub or at the boxing club.

This did not bother the leadership at the Yard. The public needed to be distracted from the everlasting scandals and the rising tide of robbery statistics as the 'Bertie Smalls Effect' wore off. The Yard bosses frequently expressed their admiration for Lundy's ingenuity. He noted the Appeal Court's objections to the Smalls supergrass experiment and came up with an improved, model prosecution. He initiated a technique for convicting men of horrendous crimes and having them jailed for decades without producing any direct evidence against them. It was a simple ploy: instead of one supergrass, Lundy's squad bred them in multiples. He backed up their allegations with confessions obtained from men in custody who had been denied access to solicitors. It was enough to convince many of the judges at the Old Bailey.

Neither the Yard nor the DPP nor the Home Office seemed to know or care that the police service was being corrupted. Lundy's section of the elite Flying Squad turned policing on its head; more and more of the very worst criminals in the land were being granted virtual immunity; other men accused of lesser crimes were being jailed for up to a quarter of a century on evidence that looks increasingly dubious as the years pass.

Lundy's first swoop came in November 1977. Early one morning his new robbery squad went to an address near Garner's mansion in Southgate and arrested David Smith, a long-time armed robber. They claimed he was planning to ambush a payroll delivery at a North London factory.

Among those arrested were old associates of Smith — Danny Gowan, Alfie Berkeley and George Williams. They all had convictions for robbery and were prime targets for the new squad. But once they were locked in the cells there was a shortage of direct evidence against them. However, when they came to trial 16 months later, for a series of nasty armed robberies in which guns had been fired and ammonia squirted, Lundy had a novel case and even more novel witnesses.

The only record of what happened in Lundy's interrogation rooms is what he and his squad wrote down. The men in the dock disputed this mound of paperwork. They insisted that the interviews in which they were said to have confessed had never taken place.

The main witness was a suddenly penitent David Smith, who had taken the supergrass deal offered by Lundy. He made statement after statement accusing his former friends of appalling robberies. He admitted taking part in dozens more himself. But there was a problem which could prevent Smith being a witness at the Old Bailey, so Lundy turned to 'Fat' George Williams and offered him the deal too.

An armoury of shotguns, pistols and ammunition had been found in the house Williams shared with his brother John. It looked as if both brothers were on their way to long spells in jail. Despite evidence that John Williams had made keys, repaired shotguns and been a vital back-up member of the gang, Lundy secured him a six-month sentence. Brother 'Fat' George was given the new, post-Bertie Smalls supergrass tariff of five years and the prosecution case was complete.

The trial of the rest of 'Smith's gang' opened at the Old Bailey in February 1979. It ran for 84 days. Judge Argyle admitted that the supergrasses Smith and Williams were 'two of the most dangerous criminals in British history' and that while he did not doubt they were telling the truth 'it was nauseating to hear these hypocrites and to reflect that as a matter of policy they have only been sentenced to five years each.'

Had more of the truth about these supergrasses been disclosed at the Old Bailey, Argyle's comments might have been even tougher. The 'evidence' against the defendants might also have been treated in a more cautious manner. They were all found guilty and Gowan and Berkeley were jailed for 25 years. Two other men were given 20 years and 15 years.

Justice was not well served when David Smith was selected to give evidence for the Crown. Of all the disreputable robbers that the Yard and the DPP produced as witnesses of truth at the Old Bailey, Smith was the least acceptable. They had all terrorised the public with guns; they had all preferred the life of outlaws. Smith was worse: there was indisputable evidence that he had bludgeoned a harmless old man to death on the streets of London and so would do and say anything to escape the penalty he deserved.

Murder was the one crime which the supergrass deal could not expunge. It seemed that there could be no immunity for Smith, so he could not become the vital state witness that Lundy needed in his first big case since taking charge at Finchley. Smith had to be cleared of the murder. Meanwhile, Lundy and his squad took copious statements and hoped that somehow Smith could get off the murder charge and into the witness box at the Old Bailey.

The murder took place in 1971 during a robbery in Shoreditch. Smith had coshed Kurt Hess, an elderly factory owner, so hard that he died in hospital three weeks later. It was only after a complaint from Hess's widow that Smith was charged. Smith was in custody making supergrass statements for nearly nine months before the DPP made a surprising discovery. A pathologist's report was produced which stated that Hess's poor health had contributed to his own death, and so the murder charge would be reduced to manslaughter. At the stroke of a pen Smith could now be a prosecution witness.

Another murder was also attributed to Smith. In 1971 bookmaker Harry Barham was found dead in a car in East London. Soon the story that Smith had shot him in the back of the head and stolen £40,000 from his corpse was doing the rounds in the pubs. Lundy's squad could not find enough evidence to charge Smith with this murder.

In court Lundy claimed that Smith's information had been 'a major breakthrough in the fight against crime'. Smith returned the courtesy, telling the *Daily Mail*, 'I expected a right duffing up when I was nicked. But that bloke Lundy is a gent.'

There was still more blood on the hands of Lundy's witnesses. In 1967 Smith and 'Fat' George Williams had kidnapped Walter Price, manager of a North London supermarket, to get the keys to the safe. The 16-stone Williams 'looked after' Mr Price by coshing him savagely on the head. His widow, Mrs Christina Price, remembers him staggering home with a lump on his head 'as big as an egg'. Price collapsed and died eight weeks later from heart failure. The police told Mrs Price that a man had been arrested and charged but did not keep their promise to let her know when the case came to court. It was years before she discovered that Williams had received the lenient supergrass sentence of five years; in reality about 30 months' detention in luxury quarters. She commented: 'That seems a very light sentence for murder.'

It was surprising that Lundy had not known more about the criminals Smith and Williams earlier. They lived and worked in the heart of his patch and some of their social connections merged with his. On the committee of the Finchley Boxing Club was Ted Williams, uncle to 'Fat' George and brother John. The son of another member of Smith and Williams's gang boxed there too. The well-informed Roy Garner was a member of the club and might have been expected to tip him off.

Billy 'The Snake' Amies was rostered to be the next candidate for packaging, polishing and sanitising for production in court. He had been named by Smith as a fellow robber but many of the men that they put in jail suspected that the two robbers had always planned to go supergrass together if they were caught.

Lundy soon discovered that Amies was in custody in the North of England awaiting trial on three charges of robbery brought by Merseyside police. These robberies, like all Amies's crimes, were carried out with vicious and gratuitous violence.

In the first robbery, a 40-year-old woman had been attacked in her caravan. She told detectives that one of the gang 'held on to my hair and continually punched me in the face'. In the second, a woman, her mongol daughter and her 29-year-old son were all tied up. The son was then told by one of the robbers, 'I'm going to cut your balls off.' In the third attack a garage owner and his family were also tied up. He remembered, 'Someone grabbed me between the legs and squeezed my testicles.'

The assailant in each case was Billy Amies. He was facing a very long sentence and nobody could offer him any way out of his predicament, until Tony Lundy arrived in Liverpool; then there was talk of a deal. Amies was taken to London for further de-briefing. The Liverpool matters were quickly dealt with. When they heard that he had gone supergrass, his two accomplices pleaded guilty and were both jailed for 15 years. Their cases were concluded on a Friday and Amies was remanded to appear in court again the following Monday, to be given a similar sentence.

Instead of being locked up for the weekend, Billy 'The Snake' was taken by his Robbery Squad minder, Detective Sergeant Bernard Craven, to the luxury of Liverpool's four-star Atlantic Towers Hotel. To while away an evening Amies took his guard to a low-life dockland pub. Their pleasant outing was destroyed when Amies was recognised as a 'grass' and attacked. Amies escaped almost unscathed through a lavatory window. Craven lost his gun and was so badly beaten that he had to be invalided out of the Met.

On the Monday it was decided to suspend sentence on Amies and allow his offences to be dealt with later at the Old Bailey. But the judge insisted that the London court should be told the details of Amies's brutal crimes and he was taken off to the welcoming arms of the North London Robbery Squad.

There should have been great concern about the reliability of their new supergrass. Amies had been discharged from the army because of his psychiatric condition and in the late 1960s underwent ECT therapy in a mental hospital. Later, in Hull prison, he was first categorised as a psychopath and paranoid schizophrenic, then as 'dangerous', and finally as 'too engrossed in himself for further examination'. While in Liverpool prison he was declared unfit to plead at his trial. This was all forgotten when Amies was required for supergrass duties. Even more about him seemed to have been forgotten in September 1978 when he appeared at the Old Bailey to receive his five years.

According to a *Daily Mirror* investigation published three years later, the court was told that a man dressed as a police officer had taken part in a number of robberies and committed several brutal acts. But, according to the *Mirror*, they were not told that the policeman was Amies, that he had carried a gun, that some of the victims had been homosexually attacked, or that Amies had a long history of mental illness. The only witness had been Tony Lundy, who told the court how Amies had given the police tremendous help. The judge told him, 'I make it plain that you have my admiration.'

That admiration might have been dulled had the judge been aware of the details of just one of Amies's crimes. In 1976 scrap dealer David Melbourne had been watching TV at his Camberley home when his 16-year-old daughter, Davina, answered the door to a man in police uniform who asked to see 'the proprietor'. As she turned to go back into the house the 'policeman' produced an iron bar and struck her across the face. Four masked men, one with a shotgun, joined the 'policeman' in the kitchen and beat her father with the iron bar before trussing up his family. The robbers then searched the house for valuables, and one of them drank a bottle of vodka which he smashed over Melbourne's head.

During the next hour Mr Melbourne was burned with a cigarette by the 'policeman' and threatened with castration. Then

Davina Melbourne, stripped to her underwear, was brought from another room and the 'policeman' asked, 'How would you like to see your daughter raped?' The gang left with about £2,000 and some jewellery. Amies was the 'policeman'. He played down his role, naming two other members of the gang as Michael Morris and Richard Smith. When that case came to trial the key evidence was provided by three of Lundy's supergrasses, Amies, David Smith and a more recent recruit, Ron Simpson.

Simpson had been arrested by Lundy and held in Brixton charged with a robbery. He was moved to 'A' wing alongside Morris who, suspecting him of being an informer, requested a prison officer to note that he was deliberately avoiding Simpson. Three months later Simpson claimed that Morris had confessed his part in the Camberley robbery to him in Brixton jail. The trial of Morris lasted two weeks. He was sentenced to 14 years, later reduced to 10 on appeal.

At his appeal in 1981 Morris's counsel described Amies as a contemptible hypocrite who had failed to tell the truth about his own crimes and was under great pressure to testify. Turning to the role of Lundy the QC said it was 'surprising' that the detective had told the judge who sentenced Amies that he was not particularly violent.

The other man named by Amies as present at the Camberley robbery was Richard Smith. He admitted an attack on a security van, but then Lundy charged him with the assault on the scrap dealer. On the basis of Amies's allegation and disputed verbal admissions he was sentenced to 15 years.

Amies served only 24 months in prison. Apart from his two fellow robbers in Liverpool who changed their pleas to guilty, he was responsible for the conviction of only three men. Little more was heard of the original claim that he had named 58 criminals or, in Lundy's words, been of 'tremendous help' to the police.

The production line was now rolling and the Yard was not slow to reward Lundy. He carried influence far in excess of his rank and, although only a DCI, was invited to attend the Yard's regular Robbery and Serious Crime conferences in the company of DACs and commanders. By 1979 the North London Robbery Squad would at any given time have up to five supergrasses located at Finchley or Whetstone — which became known as 'The Factory'. Lundy's suspects suggested this name, not because of the efficient processing of supergrasses or robbers but because they alleged it was a 'factory' where stories were manufactured.

A common factor during Lundy's supergrass era was solicitor Roland Pelly from Bishop's Stortford, who eventually acted for more than thirty of the penitents. Pelly also acted for the Lundy family, Roy Garner and several of his gang as well as for the supergrasses.

From the early 1970s Pelly represented the DPP in Hertfordshire. How it is that Pelly has acted for so many Robbery Squad supergrasses is not clear. Maybe they all felt that he was the man to get them the best deal. Some seem to have been prompted by Robbery Squad officers anxious to make sure they were dealing with a solicitor who understood the particular demands of these peculiar cases.

The supergrass phenomenon continued into the early 1980s. With every new informant paraded before the courts came the now familiar declaration that they were, again, 'the biggest breakthrough yet in the war against crime'. These early promises rarely resulted in large numbers of criminals being brought to court but the media did not go back to check the results against the earlier claims.

The press also failed to notice the essential difference between Lundy's supergrasses and their fellow criminals simultaneously being 'turned' by the Home Counties detectives at Number 5 Regional Crime Squad based at Reading. Lundy's reformed robbers did not make statements about corrupt detectives, only criminals. In contrast the 5RCS supergrasses seemed to know a great deal about money paid to London detectives and could explain why they had kept their liberty so long — until arrested by detectives outside the Met.

It was late in 1981 before the Appeal Court looked at Lundy and his supergrasses Smith and Williams. They ruled that Danny Gowan, convicted for taking part in Smith's armed robbery team, had been unlawfully arrested and 'had been overborne by oppressive conduct by the police officers charged with questioning him'. The court continued, 'Evidence obtained by oppression is not admissible and the judge has no discretion to admit it.' His sentence, and that of another man, were quashed.

Gowan served nearly four years before his appeal succeeded. Back home he had this to say about Mr Lundy: 'Lundy did have great success with his grasses, you can't take that away from him.

But the very people he's releasing he should be putting in prison. These are the people that society is saying should be locked up forever. He's putting them back on the streets again.'

Lundy's first supergrass, David Smith, negotiated his liberty in a police cell and he also died in one. The image of the reformed criminal was a sham, as Berkeley, Gowan and the others had always argued. In 1986 detectives arrested Smith as he was about to commit another armed robbery and took him to one of Lundy's old Robbery Squad police stations at Golders Green. Smith was charged with a series of robberies and so too was his fellow gunman, none other than the former Lundy supergrass Ron Simpson.

Justice belatedly caught up with Simpson: he was jailed for 21 years. There could be no second supergrass deal for David Smith either. His crimes would not be glibly written off again. His marvellous gift of remembering just what the detectives wanted to hear no longer had appeal. He cut his throat.

6 · THREE TONS OF BULLION

NOT ALL THE GUNMEN in North London felt threatened by Lundy and his supergrasses. Indeed, some of the hard core carried on robbing at their ease and then socialising with Lundy in their spare time. His 'war against crime' seemed to pass them by. But when they ambushed a lorry carrying £3.4 million-worth of silver ingots in March 1980 it turned out to be more than just Britain's biggest-ever armed robbery. The Silver Bullion affair engulfed the Yard's top thief-taker, and its biggest informer brought the payment of Britain's largest reward, the downfall of the capital's most active team of gunmen and kicked off another series of Yard corruption investigations. The Silver Bullion Robbery was a watershed for detectives and criminals of London alike.

The Samuel Montagu bullion vaults in Tooley Street on the south bank of the Thames had long been a target. They were examined first in the late 1970s by burglars who soon gave up. The depressing intelligence was that the real prize, the gold ingots, was doubly protected. Intruders would have to cut their way through the doors protecting a mountain of silver bars before turning their torches on a second set which guarded the gold.

The consensus was that while the alarm systems might be put out of action, there was not enough time in a working night to burn through to the gold. 'Cutting time' is the last line of defence of the bank and bullion vaults if their sophisticated electronic systems are compromised. The calculation is simple: the number of hours through the night that the premises are unguarded has to be exceeded by the inches per hour that the best thermic lance could cut through the toughened steel doors.

Reluctantly, the burglars withdrew. But if the building itself could not be taken, then perhaps the bullion could be intercepted in transit? The idea was touted around several teams of top-flight robbers. Roy Garner was approached, as were the Colson family of Clapton, but no one was convinced that the job would be as sweet as it sounded. But the potential prize was so great that an assault at Tooley Street could only be a matter of time.

An office manager at the haulage company was found and persuaded to pass on the dates and routes of the bullion runs. This information ended up in the capable hands of Michael 'Skinny' Gervaise, who was later described by Detective Chief Inspector Bill Peters of the Robbery Squad as 'a very, very intelligent man, probably the most intelligent criminal I have ever met'.

Gervaise is a balding, lanky six-footer, a fluent linguist and skilled burglar alarm engineer. By the age of 37, he had stolen millions from bank vaults and jewellers. His only setback was an 18-month sentence for his part in the 1975 Bank of America robbery. The proceeds of his plundering were spent on high living across Europe. One scar-faced robber, a veteran of numerous forays across the pavement, told us in awe: 'Mickey used to fly to Paris and back just for afternoon tea.'

Gervaise was intrigued by the information that tons of silver belonging to the East German government were being carried from the vaults to Tilbury docks in ordinary container lorries protected only by two unarmed guards in a saloon car. Unbelievably, the police were not warned of these runs; hours could elapse before a load would be missed. Gervaise saw the chance to steal millions. He turned to an old colleague, Mickey Sewell, to recruit the rest of the team; like him, they would all be from north of the river.

Sewell's choice as first lieutenant was Lennie Gibson, a leading London Freemason whose earnings from crime had financed a modest property empire of rented apartments throughout North London. The threat of his shotgun had generated sufficient wealth to move his wife and two daughters from a council flat in Stoke Newington to a detached house with swimming pool overlooking Bush Hill Park golf course in Enfield. He became the Master of his local Masonic lodge, The Waterways, just up the road from Garner's Cannon Lodge mansion. Alternative pleasures were provided by his Colchester-based mistress. When the strain of robbing in the city became too much, Gibson would meet her in the Queen's Head Inn at Wormingford, run at that time by a fellow Mason, or take her for winter holidays in the sun.

Gibson became the robbery organiser and the first team meeting was held in one of his properties, 171 Inderwick Road in Muswell Hill. If the walls of 171 could talk they would fill filing cabinets at the Yard's Criminal Intelligence department. Not only was the house used to store guns and burglary equipment, it had sheltered robber Billy Hickson, accidently shot by 'Colonel' George Copley during a mid-1970s hold-up. Gibson regularly used it for planning his own robberies and also as the 'slaughter' where the proceeds could be divided up.

Gervaise, Sewell and Gibson were all present at that first meeting, and so was Gibson's long-time lieutenant, Rudolpho Aguda, known to his friends as Dolph and known to the police for his habit of going on robberies with his trusty sawn-off on the end of a string lanyard. After discussing tactics they showed faith in the enterprise by each pledging £1,000 towards the cost of buying vehicles for the robbery.

A week later they met up at 171 again, when a fifth member of the team was introduced to Gervaise. This was Dolph's nephew, Renalto 'Ron' Aguda, a lorry driver whose skill at uncoupling trailers from their tractor units was crucial to the success of the hijack.

Then, as Gervaise told later, they got down to the business of armed robbery: 'A meeting was made at Inderwick Road some days later where I met Mickey, Gibson, Dolph and Ron. They had brought a police uniform with peaked cap for me to try on. Lennie Gibson had got the uniform but I don't know where from. They then discussed the way to stop the lorry. Dolph would go to the driver dressed in a white smock coat with a clipboard and inform him that it was a Ministry of Transport road check and would he switch off his engine, step down and bring his log sheets.

'When he was out of the cab and out of view from the road he was going to be forced at gunpoint to get into a van. Dolph was to have a sawn-off shotgun under his coat. At the same time, Ron, also in a white smock coat, would go to the driver of the security car and point a gun at him. This was to be a handgun which he had in a shoulder holster. When all this was discussed at this meeting I saw a black hold-all which contained a holster, a handgun and a sawn-off shotgun. I believe that they were the property of Lennie, Dolph and Ron.'

The handgun and the sawn-off had been seen many times before on the streets of London. Exactly 30 days before the Silver Bullion Robbery, less than a mile away from Inderwick Road, they were to be waved again — at a Securicor guard when Gibson, the Agudas and another robber named Billy Young took £30,000 from the Ever Ready factory in Tottenham. That morning's work did not interrupt the build-up to the bullion robbery.

Further planning meetings were held at Inderwick Road and at The Robinson Crusoe pub, close by the Islington home of Bert Devere, the driver they would soon rob. Then the information was passed that the next silver run was due and, with less than a week to go, they decided to mount the assault from a layby on the A13 at Ripple Road in Barkingside.

Only one problem remained. The prize could be as much as 20 tons of silver. What was to be done with this bulky load which, once missing, would be hunted by legions of detectives? Gervaise remembers, 'It was agreed the silver should be kept stored for about two months and it would then be put on the market by Lennie, who knew someone in Hatton Garden that he could go to.'

The execution of the robbery was so blindingly simple that the teams who turned down the work earlier must have mourned such wealth slipping through their fingers. On Monday 24 March Gervaise and Sewell drove to Ripple Road and, finding themselves the first arrivals, parked near the chosen layby soon after 10 am. Gervaise was wearing the police uniform and a false moustache. Sewell topped his false moustache with a light brown wig.

Minutes later Ron arrived in a red box van accompanied by the two mystery men of the robbery, known only as 'Mick' and 'Roger'. Gervaise has always insisted, to the amusement of the criminal world, that he did not know their identities, and the other robbers refuse to comment. Ron got into the Transit and strapped on his shoulder holster and its 'cannon-like' revolver. On top he wore his white coat. The Five waited for warning of the arrival of the bullion lorry.

The day had started badly for driver Bob Devere. He was late out of bed, late collecting his lorry from the depot, and when he got to Tooley Street he lied and said that he had been blocked by another lorry in the yard. When the police discovered later that he had been lying, it temporarily fuelled their suspicions that he must be the inside man they were looking for. Eventually, 10,000 kilos of silver were loaded into Devere's container. As he pulled out of Tooley Street the two security guards in their saloon car settled in behind the lorry for the run to Tilbury. After they had crossed to the north bank of the Thames they noticed a small Ford van with two men in it, and a couple of miles before the Ripple Road layby, the guards and Devere saw the van overtake them.

At the wheel of the Ford van was Gibson, his passenger was Dolph. At 11.10 they drew level with the rest of the robbers, now in position in their two vans in the layby. Dolph jumped out and confirmed that the bullion was minutes away. Gervaise started organising the bogus Ministry check point and caught the eye of milkman Dave Gladden who was trundling along the A13. 'He looked so funny I had to turn round and have another look.'

Just down the road from the layby, warehouse manager Kenneth Floyd, a part-time special constable, noticed the 'policeman' supervising the traffic cones being set out in the layby. 'He started pointing at the cones and it appeared to me that none of the men there seemed to know what they were doing, they were becoming excited and agitated and were not acting like a normal council gang.' Floyd also saw a man with a clipboard and noticed the bullion lorry pulling in. Then he turned back to his work.

Lorry driver Bernard Burnham was already in the layby and had to be moved on. He was approached by Ron. 'I wound down the window and he said, "Ministry check point, would you mind moving off in five minutes, mate." At the time I thought it strange as they normally do not use this layby but the next one. He kept looking round him all the time.' Burnham duly left as requested but moments later tanker driver Tom Clark pulled in at the near end of the layby. Busy catching up on his log sheets, he did not realise what was going on before his eyes.

'As I entered the layby I noticed that there were cones marking off the bottom and there was a policeman standing by them. Also at the same time there was a Ministry man wearing a white full-length coat with a donkey jacket over the top. I got on with my log sheet and kept glancing up at what was going on in front. I felt things weren't right. The policeman did not walk in the usual manner. The next time I looked up the van had gone and all that was left was a cream-coloured car and traffic cones.' The silver, the lorry, the driver, the guards and the robbers had come and gone, leaving only the abandoned security car.

The crucial gamble of the robbery was that driver Devere would respect Gervaise's police uniform. The robber was convincing enough. 'I stepped out into the main Ripple Road and when the lorry was about 20 yards from me, I pointed at it and waved the vehicle into the layby. The driver followed my instruction, braked hard and pulled over to the layby followed by the security car. Dolph and Sewell, later joined by Ron, went to the driver of the lorry. The driver of the security vehicle got out of the car and started to approach me. I told him to speak to the Ministry officials.

'I walked to the red box van and told Roger that the others might need some help; he then walked down the layby behind the two security men. Lennie stayed in the Ford van in case we needed to get away quickly. I could see that Dolph was holding the shotgun at the men and Ron was there but he had his back to me. Roger had joined the group and was watching. Sewell, Dolph, Ron and Roger put the men in the back of the Transit. Dolph then went to the security car and moved it a few yards so it was parked properly. He then joined Gibson in the white van. Ron drove the lorry away and Dolph and Lennie followed it.' Bob Devere remembers being told, as he was hustled into the back of Gervaise's Transit, 'I'll blow your kneecaps off if you don't stay still.' The guards were threatened similarly. The silver had changed hands.

Gervaise then drove the Transit van away to Greenwich Park, with Sewell and Roger in the back guarding their three prisoners. He waited an hour to give the others time to get away from

Barking and drive the silver to Ron's haulage yard in Walthamstow for the 'slaughter'. Gervaise then went on to Deptford and found a lock-up garage on a council estate. With Sewell and Roger he forced the door, pushed in the three men and secured them with a padlock and chain. They dropped Roger off at the Elephant and Castle and abandoned the Transit in nearby Balfour Street.

Later that night Gervaise, Sewell, Gibson and Dolph met outside the Finsbury Park Tavern in North London. Gibson complained that he had lost half a stone in weight unloading the ten metric tons of silver from the stolen container. They met again the following day and agreed not to touch their prize for two months until the heat had died down. Gervaise then turned his mind to his next piece of work, 22 days hence, when he was going to rob a Hatton Garden jewellery firm of £800,000-worth of stones. Gibson and Dolph later moved the silver ingots to Gibson's long-time secret store, a rented lock-up garage near Oakwood station, where the suburbs meet the Hertfordshire countryside and where he usually kept the police uniform and guns. Only those two knew where it was hidden and they kept a key each.

7 · JUST A BUNCH OF AMATEURS

FIFTY DAYS PASSED before the Flying Squad got their break-through in the hunt for the silver. The seeds of their success had been sown the previous year when Mickey Sewell was arrested at Lennie Gibson's house in Inderwick Road. Outside was a stolen car with key-cutting equipment, masks and other burglary tools destined for use on a Birmingham jeweller's. Sewell was on the run at the time of his arrest, wanted for his role in planning a £200,000 wages snatch.

He was arrested by Detective Chief Inspector Bill Peters, who was chasing a team of armed robbers led by Ronnie 'Brains' Johnson. Peters's offer to Sewell was blunt: he would have to be charged with the payroll job and possessing the burglary kit but he could have bail if he would infiltrate the Johnson gang. The deal was accepted and Sewell went to work. If he could hand over Johnson's body then he had a chance of escaping a long sentence. Within days Johnson had learned of the scheme.

The inevitable confrontation took place in a Holloway drinking club. Johnson tracked Sewell down to the bar and asked him one direct question. The room went quiet; everybody understood the code. Had he recently got bail, enquired Johnson. Sewell confirmed that was the case. Then, according to ritual, Johnson asked, 'Is there anything you want to tell me?' Sewell also knew the code; he should have owned up to the trade with detective

Peters but assured Johnson that he had no intention of grassing anybody. It was the wrong answer and Sewell was right-hooked across the bar and denounced as 'a filthy fucking grass'.

Sewell swallowed this and, ten days after being freed by Peters, robbed the Birmingham jewellers of £230,000 worth of watches. He also kept his ear to the ground. The Robbery Squad pumped its other informers, and on 12 May 1980, the police were lying in wait for the Johnson gang. Their target was a cash delivery to a bank in East Finchley. The Squad's information was slightly inaccurate; they had staked out the wrong bank, and the first they knew of the robbery was a radio message that a guard had been gunned down a couple of blocks away.

The gang escaped, but not for long. They were tracked down within hours, and one of the team, Chris Wren, who modestly described himself as a market stall-holder's assistant, was arrested, crumbled quickly and grabbed at Lundy's offer of the supergrass deal. He was jailed for five years by Judge Leonard, who said, 'I shall take into account your intention to go straight in the future.' Wren was back at the Old Bailey almost as soon as he finished his brief spell in prison, this time admitting burglary. Johnson and the rest of the gang received long sentences.

Lundy told the court, in his well-worn phrase, that Wren's information was the 'biggest breakthrough yet in the war against crime'. The court was also told the touching story of why Wren was ready to turn his back on crime. Apparently he had decided on one last big job to pay for a 'society-style wedding'. A long-time associate of Wren told us: 'What a load of bollocks! Chrissie Wren was a degenerate. He always used to go with prostitutes. He picked this "brass" up one night in Kings Cross and took a fancy to her and brought her to live with him. He used to bash her about and she was probably highly relieved the night he got nicked.'

One of the names Wren gave up was that of a burglar from Islington, Tony Fiori. Like Sewell he had avoided any serious sentence over the years by supplying information to the police. Equally quickly, Fiori opted to become a supergrass, and the most important name he gave up was that of Mickey Gervaise. Fiori revealed that Gervaise had two 'tame' burglar alarm engineers on his payroll. They were paid weekly retainers and a percentage from each successful job for helping bypass the alarms on banks and jewellers' premises in Hatton Garden.

Wren and Fiori had 'gone crooked' so fast that the Squad lifted 'Skinny' Gervaise only six days after the Finchley shooting. On 18 May 1980 Gervaise was taken to Enfield police station but refused to talk for four days. He knew well enough that all the detectives had against him was the testimony from Fiori.

When left alone in a cell with Fiori for a few minutes Gervaise guaranteed him £25,000 to retract. To his horror Fiori went straight to his police handlers and reported the offer! Later Gervaise would grumble that Fiori was 'more of a cozzer than the cozzers'. But the screw was tightening: the alarm company engineers were arrested, confessed, and now there was corroboration. Gervaise confided to us later: 'First there was one, then two, then three against me. I couldn't believe it. I was facing 15 years and they didn't even know about the silver.'

Chief Inspector Peters spent 12 days 'chatting' to Gervaise and in due course he sacked his solicitor and engaged the services of Roland de voeux Pelly. He started to talk, but only named a fraction of his crimes, ignoring both the recent Hatton Garden and Silver Bullion robberies.

The Yard tried to keep its latest supergrass secret so that men being named did not take immediate vacations in Spain, but, as the first arrests of his fellow burglers began, the news that Mickey 'has gone over' seeped out. One suspect, being escorted through Enfield police station, saw Chief Inspector Peters with his arm around Gervaise's shoulders. Realising what had happened, he told his wife on her next visit to put the word out, and the first person she rushed to warn was Lennie Gibson.

It was late May and Gibson was relaxing by his pool. To her surprise he seemed unmoved by this catastrophic news. Not only was Gibson confident that Gervaise would never reveal his involvement in the bullion job, he also felt certain that his friend Roy Garner would alert him if the police were planning to swoop. But this time the alliance between Gibson and Garner, which went back two decades, could not hold. An insurance reward of £300,000 had been advertised and Garner's greed won out. He had to strike first before Gervaise could admit the robbery, surrender the silver and so deny Garner the reward.

Having previously turned down the chance to join the team of robbers going after the silver, Garner always knew who had done it. The scramble for the reward was on, Lundy and Garner conferred, and a meeting was set up on the night of Friday 30 May with no less a figure than DAC David Powis. It was essential that Powis heard the information from Garner if he was going to be persuaded to endorse the recommendation to pay such a huge reward.

Lundy struck as Gervaise was resting in his cell at Enfield. Five years later, in a prison visiting room, Gervaise told us his version of what happened. 'It was a Saturday afternoon and Lundy came in on his day off. He said, "Sit there, don't say anything, just listen to me. Something very big has gone." He knew every detail about the business, he knew everything, it was as if he had been a fly on the wall.'

The only version we have of what was said during the next few crucial days are Lundy's written records and the eventual confession of his long-time drinking companion, Lennie Gibson. These statements are presented in the unreal and stilted language that detectives and criminals use when they have to put a public face on their private world. Years on, they read like the script for a mannered, drawing-room farce.

Initially Lundy arrived in the cell with Superintendent Reg Dixon. Gervaise asked him to leave the room so that he and Lundy could speak privately. Dixon left them alone saying, 'I'll go and order some teas.' Then, according to Lundy's version of events, Gervaise said he was worried about causing personal problems for Lundy. The detective riposted, 'I will have no hesitation in arresting anyone who has been involved in villainy — have no doubt about that. It doesn't matter to me how serious — if someone I know has been involved in crime they will be treated in the same way as anybody else.'

Gervaise then announced dramatically, 'It involves Lennie.' Again Lundy went into the public address mode, 'Get one thing straight. Lennie is a likeable type but I have no allegiances to him or anyone else. If they are involved in villainy they will be nicked and dealt with like anyone else.'

Gervaise persisted, 'But I thought he was a very good friend of yours.' 'No way,' said Lundy, forgetting the pictures taken years before of himself with Gibson and Garner, 'I have known him socially from drinking in the same pub — but we are no more friends than that.' Gervaise still hesitated, as if trying to help Lundy. 'I understand you were in the same Lodge as him.' This Lundy denied absolutely, 'I have never had anything to do with Freemasonry. Obviously somebody has frightened you by suggesting associations and friendships which don't exist.'

Once this highly moral set of announcements was at an end, Gervaise revealed, 'I was on the Silver Bullion job with Lennie Gibson.' Timing Lundy's version of the conversation against a stopwatch, it appears that Gervaise, the master criminal with long experience of police interrogations, capitulated in the space of 90 seconds. Coincidentally, the senior officer returned with the teas and Lundy said, 'Now I understand — tell Mr Dixon about it.' Dixon interjected, 'I've known Mr Lundy for many years and he has nothing to fear,' and so Gervaise began his disclosures.

Gervaise started naming the robbers and Lundy intervened. 'Mickey Sewell is already on bail and must be worried sick in case you are grassing him. We will have to step in a bit quick before they all abscond — if they haven't done already.' Sewell, always a liability because of his fear of a heavy sentence, had disappeared the previous day, after being warned by Garner.

Gervaise began dictating his confession about the Bullion Robbery at 6pm on the Saturday evening. It continued through the next day and was completed on Monday afternoon. Gibson and Dolph Aguda were arrested together at gunpoint on Tuesday and Gibson was taken to Golders Green police station. He was interviewed from 6.45 until 7.10 pm, alone, by Lundy.

The detective's record of the interview begins on a matey note. 'Haven't seen you for some time now Len, I didn't expect to be meeting you again under these circumstances — but I'm afraid you've got big problems facing you.' Touchingly, Gibson replied, 'I don't expect any favours — you've got your job to do — I know you do it well — spell it out to me — where do I stand, what's it all about?'

Lundy confirmed it was the Silver Bullion Robbery and urged him, 'Throw yourself at the mercy of the court and hope you can mitigate yourself in that way and get a reasonable sentence. You must be mad — you have a bit of history — and then you put it all behind you — work hard and set up a business — have a good living coming in and then get involved in something like this.'

Gibson was quick to pick up the cue. He confessed immediately. 'Its no good me crying over spilt milk, but don't you think I know what a cunt I've been — we didn't even know what to do with it when we got it.' Lundy batted this straight back to Gibson, 'I can't give promises but I'm sure it would be taken into account if you gave it all back — if you were tempted after years of working hard to straighten out your life, you must hope for a reasonable sentence.' Gibson agreed and added another brush stroke to his picture of remorse, 'There is no danger I will ever get involved in anything ever again as long as I live.' The interview only lasted 2.5 minutes, leaving 22.5 minutes unaccounted for. According to Lundy, after Gibson's dramatic admission of being on the biggest ever robbery in Britain, 'there then followed a conversation about family and domestic matters'.

An hour later Gibson saw Lundy again and enquired about his freedom. 'Do you think there will be any chance of bail? I wouldn't run away — I know I'm going to prison — I would just like to sort out a few business problems for my wife before I go away.' Lundy, on the record, made it clear that he would oppose bail. Subsequently Gibson won bail.

Gibson still refused to reveal where the prize was hidden and demanded to see Dolph. At 9pm Lundy, Gibson and Dolph Aguda confronted Detective Superintendent David Little. Wisely, Little set out the ground rules. 'I want you to understand that I am in charge of this inquiry and I will make decisions and I want to know everything that is going on.'

Nevertheless Gibson asked if he and Dolph could be alone with Lundy. Little refused. Gibson again tried to take charge, still playing the trump card that only he and Dolph knew where the silver was. 'Look Tony, you know what I'm trying to do — you know I won't pull any strokes — no disrespect to you Mr Little but I don't think he will talk in your presence whereas he knows that I have known Tony for many years and I think he will realise that he can be trusted.'

Lundy then took over and signalled to Aguda how the story could be told, if he would play along. 'A strong temptation was put to you both — you have a bit of history the two of you and in spite of that you've worked hard and built up businesses — unfortunately you didn't resist temptation and went along with organising a major robbery.' The debate went on and so Gibson appealed again.

'Listen Mr Little, no disrespect to you but please leave us alone with Mr Lundy — I'm not trying to pull any strokes — but it will be easier to talk to Dolph with just Mr Lundy present — I know you think something funny is going on — but there isn't — it's just that I know him personally — and trust him.' Little then agreed. 'I will go and have a cup of tea and see you shortly.' During the following two hours Lundy, Gibson and Dolph Aguda bargained in private. There is no record of what was said. Meanwhile the silver was lying unprotected in a garage just four miles from the police station.

Late that night Aguda and Gibson agreed to write confessions. But there was one more problem: eventually it would bring in the anti-corruption squad. The first clue came from Aguda. 'We will admit we have done it and give the property back — I think it's all there, will it reflect on us if there is some missing?' Lundy jumped in. 'If you are honestly trying to give it back I'm certain it will be taken into account at Court — if someone else has taken some there's not much you can do about it.' He added the final brush stroke to the picture: 'I'm not the judge but I would think you must expect seven years at least, but I can't guarantee you anything.'

Lundy and other officers then took Gibson off to the lock-up garage. The door had to be forced and 309 bars were recovered. Twelve were missing. Why the detectives were unable to open the door with ease is one of the many mysteries of the Silver Bullion saga. When arrested both Gibson and Aguda had keys in their possession.

Gibson was taken back to dictate his confession. He made himself sound like an amateur. 'When I say I was involved, I didn't go on the actual job, and use guns. I've been in trouble in the past with the law but that was ten years ago, it was over something stupid. I realised that I wasn't getting any younger, I had a fantastic wife and two lovely daughters and didn't want to put them through the ordeal of visiting me in prisons and calling at police stations for me. I bought a couple of old houses and smashed them about and made something of them. I sold them at a profit, used that money to buy other property, renovate it and re-sell it and gradually built myself up to the situation where I've now a number of flats which I rent out which supports me and my family comfortably.

'Now to explain how I became involved in this bullion job which you must know from your own experience got out of all proportion and resulted in me not having very much sleep over the last 11 weeks and believe me, that's the truth. I know it might sound silly to you but I don't like being disloyal to anybody so if you don't mind, I won't mention the names of others involved. I was approached by a certain party who asked me if I was interested in earning a nice few bob, the job was explained to me several times before I eventually gave in to the temptation of easy money again. It seemed so simple that I could hardly believe that a lorry with such a valuable load was not escorted properly. One of the conditions when the job was talked about was that there was not going to be any violence, no one was going to get hurt.

'When I eventually found out how much the silver was worth I was shocked to think that we had pulled up something we had never expected to be so valuable. After that things just got out of all proportion. It was only a matter of time before the stuff had to go back to its rightful owners but no one could pluck up enough courage to move it and make the necessary phone call so that it could be found.

'Have you ever been in that sort of position where you don't know which way to turn and don't know what to do for the best and at the same time you want to kick yourself for getting involved. To the best of my knowledge all that silver is intact, none of it has been moved, not even a sample. You must have met plenty of villains in your time to know that we're not hardened thieves, it was a silly venture that suddenly got out of all proportion and cost me money personally. My only consolation is that you've got the silver back.'

That was the end of the investigation. Neither Gibson nor the Agudas have ever revealed the true identities of 'Mick' and 'Roger', the source that supplied them with a genuine police uniform for the robbery or where they have hidden the guns. The Yard held a press conference to show off the recaptured bullion and nobody seemed to worry very much about the 12 missing bars, valued at about £120,000. It would be nearly seven months before the robbers came to court for sentence. In the meantime, things were not so bad for them. Despite still being in possession of the guns they were given bail.

Would the Old Bailey judge who sentenced them be taken in by the nonsense about Gibson being a reformed character who had turned his back on crime for the previous decade? The three robbers went to the Old Bailey in January 1981 in considerable trepidation. Naturally, Lundy was available to assist with the mitigation pleas. A senior Yard detective told us about that day. He said, 'Word quickly spread around the Yard about what Lundy had said. We couldn't believe it and we couldn't believe that he would be allowed to get away with it. But he did.'

Lundy had been head of the North London Robbery Squad and privy to the vast information the Criminal Intelligence branch had about the robbers on his patch. He would have in his desk, and be an important contributor to, a secret file known among the detectives as 'The Top 100'. This listed the most dangerous, active, armed robbers in London and gave details about their associates. We were the first journalists to obtain a copy of this file. The list is drawn up in alphabetical order. Number 42 is Leonard John Gibson. Just prior to the Silver Bullion Robbery it listed Gibson's criminal speciality as armed robbery and named Dolph Aguda as one of his close associates. Judge Miskin, about to pass sentence, would be unaware of this confidential Yard document and could only be guided by the picture that Lundy painted of Gibson.

Lundy said that he had known the gunman for a dozen years through the Finchley Boxing Club and stressed 'Gibson was a supporter at the various functions, more on a charitable basis.' Lundy then declared, 'As far as I knew he was a successful businessman who had put his past behind him. I had no idea he was involved in criminal matters.' Gibson's counsel asked if there was any evidence at all of Gibson's involvement in any sort of crime in recent years. 'There is no evidence to support any question of him being involved, no.'

Lundy continued, offering a family sketch. 'I saw his wife shortly after his arrest and I know the effect on them all was of shock and surprise that he was involved in crime.' The lawyers finished off the pleas by describing the gang as 'amateurs of crime' who were out of their depth with such a huge prize. The judge seemed impressed and Gibson and the Agudas relaxed; they were getting the deal. Miskin concluded, 'Each of you is genuinely remorseful and the sentence I have passed is significantly reduced.' Then, pointedly ignoring the signals in the statements, he jailed each for ten years, much less than the normal penalty but much more than they expected.

Stunned, the three were put down. Back at the Yard a report from Tony Lundy was working its way through the bureaucracy. It recommended that his informant 'Dave Granger' be paid the £300,000 insurance reward.

8 · OPERATION ALBANY

THE YARD PICKED the wrong detective when it chose Harry Clement to investigate Roy Garner. It knew he would be determined to discover the truth but it relied on the fact that he was a loyal officer. If its delicate relationship with Garner was likely to cause embarrassment then, it hoped Clement could be depended on not to rock the boat. In the years to come the Yard discovered, to its horror, that Clement would put his duties as a policeman before the political interests of the leadership.

Clement joined the Met in 1959, following his service in the Grenadier Guards. He became a career detective and rose slowly up the ranks, working on the Flying Squad and most of the other elite teams. He was involved in the hunt for the Kray Twins and was one of the first detectives on the scene of the IRA shootout at Balcombe Street. He was at the Spaghetti House siege and also conducted long investigations into the Mafia in Britain. In 1966 he was awarded the British Empire Medal for gallantry after being temporarily blinded with ammonia while trying to arrest two violent thieves. Clement, by then a detective superintendent, was rated on both sides of the fence as shrewd and totally incorruptible.

The biggest and last challenge of his career came as Gibson and his gang were awaiting sentence for the Silver Bullion

Robbery and Garner and Lundy were looking forward to the payment of the huge reward. The catalyst was a North London armed robber named John Moriarty, who had asked to be treated as a supergrass. Moriarty had survived two shotgun attacks from fellow villains but could not face a long spell in prison. In September 1980 Clement was ordered to head the team which would investigate Moriarty's claims. The detective was no enthusiast for the supergrass system and was only too well aware of its potential for abuse. From the outset Clement instructed his squad that every allegation must be substantiated by independent corroboration.

Moriarty's decision to turn supergrass was a major blow to Garner and his friends at the Yard. Past investigations had been blocked at early stages by the middle-ranking officers protecting him. The Moriarty allegations deftly evaded these barriers and went to the top. His status as a resident informant also meant that there would be independent investigations and reports going outside the Met to the DPP.

Clement's squad based itself at Albany Street police station, near Regent's Park, named itself 'Operation Albany', and got to work. Clement chose Chief Inspector Gerry Wiltshire as his deputy and between them they hand-picked a team which at full strength numbered 45 detectives.

Albany started up in the autumn of 1980 as Lundy was making headlines again at the Old Bailey with another of his reformed criminals, armed robber Tony Azzopardi. After hearing Lundy's usual set-piece speech about the gunman's 'big breakthrough in the war against armed robbery' the judge called him 'a brave man' and handed down the tariff of five years for 49 robberies. Two weeks later Lundy was promoted to Superintendent. True to pattern, Azzopardi's next public appearance was at Snaresbrook Crown Court in 1986, where he was jailed for burglary. DAC Powis also met twice with Garner before Christmas to hand him two rewards which totalled more than £40,000. This was not disclosed to Clement.

Clement had not previously investigated Garner but he had heard of him. In early 1980, when Clement was deputy head of the Met's Regional Crime Squad, he received disturbing intelligence from junior officers. They told him that one of his detective sergeants, Peter Docherty, was shooting over land at

Wormley belonging to a major target criminal by the name of Roy Garner. Clement recalls now, 'It was important to me that as honest, loyal officers, they had spotted something wrong and wished to rectify it.' He immediately ordered that a file be made up from Garner's criminal intelligence records. He took one look at it and immediately summoned Docherty.

Clement was adamant; Docherty must cease all dealings with Garner. To Clement's surprise he found Docherty's attitude 'truculent and unprofessional' and decided to have him posted off the Squad. Had Clement known that Docherty kept a caravan at Holborn Stud Farm and knew a great deal about Garner and his guns, he might have sought stronger action.

Operation Albany got into its stride in the New Year. Garner had been tipped off that he was being targeted but after so many years of protection he was not about to change his ways. In January he swung into action to end a tenancy at Kenny Ross's Tudor Farm next to his own Holborn Stud at Wormley. Specifically, an axe was swung hard one night at the leg of a horse. It was just the first in a series of threats.

Theresa Tickler is a slim, blonde horsewoman who now lives far from London. In 1978 she signed a lease with one of Garner's solicitors, Harold Margolis, and then attracted 25 clients and their horses to the livery stables. In February 1981 Garner suddenly gave her two weeks to leave. It was the culmination of a campaign of harassment that was regularly reported to the local police.

Valuable horses were let out of stables and paddocks. Gates were left open and rocks thrown while horses were being exercised. Shotguns were fired at night outside a caravan in which her staff tried to keep watch and cartridges were left in the horses' bedding. The ignition system in a horsebox was turned on and left to burn out. One intruder came at dusk and brazenly climbed on the stable roof after letting a horse out. Tickler quickly gave in. She told us, 'I could have stayed but I left because I was frightened for myself, my staff and my horses. I had heard what had happened to a previous tenant and also I was visited by Garner's son Mark and given a countdown of the days I had left at Tudor Farm.'

The campaign against Ms Tickler was a re-run of an earlier illegal eviction of a tenant at Tudor Farm. Moriarty told Operation Albany about it. Ross and Garner had inherited

Sandra Mann as a sitting tenant when they took over the premises in April 1976. Two years later Ross suddenly gave her notice to quit. She took legal advice, and when Ross found out he told her he was 'very annoyed' and that he would get her out of Tudor Farm whatever it cost him. Soon afterwards burglars smashed through a steel-lined door and stole £3,000 worth of tack. Sandra Mann re-equipped and tried to carry on, despite increasing pressure from Ross to go. Six weeks later her barn was burned down and she lost a horsebox and hay valued at £7,000. The next day Garner turned up and drove around her yard 'with a big smile on his face'. She left.

Tudor Farm was let briefly to various friends of Garner and Ross. Then Theresa Tickler agreed her tenancy. Her eviction occurred after Operation Albany had commenced and it was only a month later that she was interviewed by its detectives. Already Moriarty's allegations were being backed up by witnesses and independent confirmation. This was just the beginning.

Islington was fast becoming one of the more desirable parts of London. Through the 1970s the estate agents' shops spread along Upper Street as the N1 area glowed with gentrification. Roy Garner noted the arrival of the stripped pine shops, saw the rents soaring and moved in for his own killing. He bought properties cheap because they had tenants in place and then called in the arsonist who was so successful in the countryside.

Opposite the Town Hall and within view of the police station was a terrace of Georgian buildings. Or rather there had been, until the mid-70s. Early in 1973 Garner had purchased number 179 and planned to convert it into high-rent offices. But there was an obstacle: a long-established butcher, Mr Stephens, had a secure tenancy.

Over a drink one night Kenny Ross told fellow gunman Billy Young that they had tried all ways to buy Stephens out, but they couldn't remove him, and in the end they had to burn him out. On the night of 12 December 1975 eight fire engines were called to the blaze at 179; Stephens's business was ruined and the building demolished.

Next for the Garner treatment was optician Albert Arnold, whose family had run their practice next door at number 178 for half a century. Garner bought the building and told Arnold that the three floors above him would have to be demolished. If Arnold felt this was too much, he was welcome to leave. Arnold declined, summoned the district surveyor and together they stood on the steps of the Town Hall and watched Garner's men dropping rubble on top of his ceiling. He remembers the attitude of the demolition workers. 'They were frankly amazed that I was still here, and it was obvious to them, in fact they told me, "somebody's trying to get you out". It was so bad that I didn't really think I could carry on. Since that day I don't think my health has ever been the same.'

The war of attrition was increased. The arsonist was re-employed twice in the next five weeks, and the demolition workers, while trying to cave in Arnold's ceiling, conveniently dropped a wall on top of the adjoining building, number 177. Within days Garner offered, unsuccessfully, to buy it cheaply. Two arson attacks followed but the landlord was immovable. Garner and Ross decided to sell numbers 178 and 179. They made a profit of £84,000.

Moriarty's allegations continued to check out. The fire brigade confirmed that there had been a systematic campaign of arson against tenants in Upper Street in premises owned or coveted by Garner. Moriarty then revealed the name of the arsonist and that of his assistant with the matches. They had been busy all over North London.

Garner wanted more car parking facilities for Elton's disco in Tottenham and he set his sights on a house and land opposite the club which were owned by Haringey Council. There were three arson attacks in 46 days but, although considerable damage was caused, the Councillors did not get the message and the campaign was abandoned. During one of these incursions the assistant arsonist thoughtlessly threw a match on the paraffin before getting clear. He was engulfed in flames and later in bandages, and won himself the soubriquet among the Garner gang of 'the invisible man'.

When Operation Albany learned the chief fire-raiser's name they raided his home, but they were too late — he had fled to California. Clement and Wiltshire were convinced that, if they could interrogate him, he would confess and implicate Garner and Ross, and then Albany would have its breakthrough. A request was submitted for permission to travel to California. It was denied by the Yard on the grounds of expense.

Clement asked the FBI to help. They sent an agent round to the address at Laguna Beach who made clumsy inquiries about 'an Englishman'. The arsonist fled again. Later solicitor Pelly contacted the Yard, offering the fugitive for interview. This was declined.

There was one more fire to be investigated. In the early months of 1980 a new disco called Lazers, which was likely to rival Elton's, was due to open in Green Lanes, Haringey. Two men from Elton's turned up and asked to be shown round. The night before the opening the club was broken into, petrol sprinkled and set alight.

Back in Upper Street the intimidation continued in a different but equally unpleasant way. There was a warehouse on the site of number 179 and Garner rented it to a new business called Suitesville which sold elegant leather furniture. After 18 months Garner invited Suitesville to buy the property, at an inflated price, or get out. They declined. On 27 June 1980, £20,000 worth of leather furniture was delivered to the warehouse. The next day the manager, Bob Barratt, arrived at work to find the building had been burgled and everything stolen. But Barratt still refused to leave.

Garner and Ross, who had always held keys to the warehouse, changed the locks and ringed it with barbed wire. Barratt and his partners went to the High Court and won back possession. Then the threatening phone calls started and soon Suitesville was forced to leave. Weeks later the missing furniture was found at Wells Farm in Cuffley, the home of Garner's associate Stevie Salter. Curiously, Islington CID did not press Salter to explain from whom he had obtained the furniture.

Barratt was celebrating his birthday when he was arrested, taken to Islington police station and accused of stealing the furniture. He was kept in a cell overnight and, he alleges, assaulted by a detective when he refused to confess.

Another nine months were to pass before action was taken against Salter. When Albany came on the scene they took over the investigation and charged him with receiving stolen property. Later he was acquitted in dubious circumstances. Garner bribed at least one witness and word was spread that 'if Salter goes, we all go'. Clement's deputy, Gerry Wiltshire, added the case to his list under 'conspiracy to pervert the course of justice' and decided to target Salter.

Murder was the next allegation from Moriarty. The police already knew the bare facts of the case. In November 1976 a small-time criminal, Raymond Hoy, had been knifed to death in the Eureka Tavern, a Greek Restaurant in Haringey. A year later John Arthur Webb stood trial at the Old Bailey for Hoy's murder. The court heard that vital clues had been cleaned up by the restaurant staff and that a crucial witness had disappeared. After two days the judge ruled there was insufficient evidence and Webb was discharged. Webb was better known as Johnny Brixton, an armed robber and Garner's hired muscle at Elton's.

Operation Albany re-investigated the murder and found the 'missing witness'. He was Gerry Knight, a fraudster and car thief. He had been in the Eureka and saw exactly what happened. He gave Albany signed statements. According to Knight, Garner and Ross had been in the restaurant. After they left, in the early hours, there was a quarrel and Brixton stabbed Hoy to death. Knight went into hiding on the South coast because he did not want to get involved but shortly after the murder Garner, Ross and one of their gang, Mickey Sanderson, caught up with him. Their message was blunt: if the police found him he was not to name the murderer. If he did not keep his mouth shut, they would tell the police that he, Knight, was the murderer.

When we confronted Sanderson in the late spring of 1985 he admitted going on the trip to Brighton and also boasted to us about Garner and his corrupt dealings with a Yard detective. But, Sanderson declared, nothing could ever be proved about the Eureka murder 'because Vasas is dead'. Vasas Avraamides was one of the Greek-Cypriots who helped carry Hoy's body out on to the pavement and then washed the bloodstains off the floor. There remain at least two more witnesses to the murder who were threatened by Garner and will not sign statements.

There was another even more frightened witness, and when they got to her, Johnny Brixton's friends were ruthless. Albany found her, later. She had been in the Eureka the night of the murder and had left because of the ferocity of the argument between Hoy and Brixton. She and Hoy worked for Garner's associate Stevie Salter at his Edmonton offices, and when she heard of Hoy's death, two days later, she was distraught. Neighbours in her block of flats called the police and she made a statement, naming Brixton. Although he was in hiding, the news quickly reached his friends.

A few days later there was a knock on her door and three men forced their way in. In the spring of 1985, she told us what happened: 'One of them said "You've been talking and you shouldn't have," and while the other two held me, he punched me several times in the face. One of my eyes was closed up for two weeks. Then he burned me about eight times on the chest with a cigarette. They told me to go back to the police and change my statement or I would get worse. They told me to change the description of the man who was arguing with Raymond Hoy. So I did, I was too frightened to do anything else.'

She also knows the man who tortured her, whom she describes as 'a criminal I've seen drinking in Roy Garner's pub in Tottenham'. Terrified, and with one eye bruised purple and closed, she went back to the police and said she wanted to change her statement. The detectives charged her with wasting police time. Fourteen years later the scars from the cigarette burns can still be seen when she pulls down the top of her jumper.

When Brixton was acquitted of the murder there were allegations that money had 'gone in' to the detectives. Brixton sold a plot of land he owned at Cuffley, worth £19,000, and gave the proceeds to Garner to be passed on. Brixton's fear was not so much being jailed for the murder but the length of sentence he might get once a judge learned of his record. He had been charged with murder in 1970 for stabbing a man to death in Hackney, and was lucky to escape with a short sentence for manslaughter.

Five years after Hoy's death, Albany had the tortured woman witness and they had Gerry Knight. Now there was corroboration for nearly all of Moriarty's allegations, and reports were prepared for senior officers and the DPP. The Albany detectives had no doubt that they had enough to charge Garner, Ross and a number of their gang. The team were feeling bullish and they told Harry Clement, 'Governor, we've got a cast-iron one here.'

They were wrong. The DPP declined to prosecute. For all the enthusiasm and dedication of the detectives, the investigation was fatally flawed from the start. Clement is adamant that Operation Albany should have been told that Garner was a major informant and that Lundy had intimate knowledge about the criminal. But Clement was never told of Garner's double life. Lundy was neither to be of assistance, nor, when he heard of the investigation, did he volunteer any help.

During the Albany probe Clement had a visit from a senior officer. Clement recalls that in the course of a rambling conversation he was told that the bosses wanted prior knowledge of any plan to arrest Garner. Clement's response was blunt and later he let it be known that if he felt his investigations were being interfered with he would go immediately to the Commissioner or outside the Met to the Chief Inspector of Constabulary.

In November 1981 the Met closed Albany down, leaving the witnesses who had had the courage to make statements about the gangster completely unprotected. Clement said later: 'I can only echo the comments of my team. They were disgusted, they were frustrated, and I had to spend time to lift their spirits again because they, like myself, thought they had a case that ought to go before a court.' Among the detectives on Operation Albany, Garner had become known as 'Mr not to be proceeded with'. Albany was quietly disbanded and, in Clement's words, his team 'scattered to the four winds'.

This was kept secret; it was known only to a handful of detectives, and of course Roy Garner. Nine months later London Labour MP Chris Price wrote to the Attorney General asking what was happening about Garner and Ross. Sir Michael Havers, who could only rely on the briefing supplied by the Yard, replied in all innocence that 'the two men are the subject of intensive police enquiries'. That was not true because, of course, the investigation had been closed down. Garner had escaped again and Parliament and the Attorney General had been lied to.

The Yard deceived the Attorney General but Price's question in the House forced it to re-open the inquiry. Clement was away on a course at Bramshill police college in Hampshire in September 1982 when he received a visit from a senior officer. Would he re-open the Albany Inquiry on his return to London? Clement replied that he 'would not do a whitewash'.

Nevertheless Clement reconstituted the rump of his old team, but within months a recurrence of a severe injury received years earlier when arresting violent criminals forced him into hospital and then out of the Met.

The point of Albany Phase Two has eluded both observers and the small team of detectives who worked on it. Gerry Wiltshire, who took over the inquiry when Clement retired, insists that they were starved of resources. The feeling was that although Albany would never make any progress, neither the DPP, nor the Home Office, nor the Yard could admit publicly that they had abandoned investigations into Garner and Ross. Privately, corrupt detectives burgled Albany's safe at the Yard and its lockers in Tottenham Court Road Police Station.

Garner was kept well informed of what was going on and, far from running away from the detectives, he sought to confront them. He was well aware that he was watched by a Special Intelligence team. One afternoon, in Muswell Hill, he decided to give them a taste of their own medicine. Carefully noting the numbers of the vehicles following him, he pulled his light van into a pub car park and phoned a police friend. Garner waited while the numbers were checked, proved to be Met undercover surveillance vehicles, and then drove off.

Minutes later he slammed on his brakes and reversed into the grey van to his rear. Jumping out, he confronted the embarrassed policeman who was sitting at the wheel with a radio-microphone strapped to his chest. Grinning hugely, Garner drove off. Within hours a protest letter from his solicitor Roland Pelly was on its way to the Met.

Albany was not closed down again; the Yard was content that the officers most determined to capture Garner should soldier on until they retired.

9 · THE ROAD TO TOTHILL STREET

TONY LUNDY did his best to sabotage Operation Albany. Without Harry Clement's knowledge, Lundy went over his head to their boss, DAC David Powis, and tried to undermine the allegations against Garner. When Clement found out, he was outraged. Lundy had no right to protect the criminal from police investigations.

From the earliest days of Operation Albany, Powis had been meeting Garner in secret to pay him rewards. Handing over money in person was one of Powis's initiatives to cut down on corruption surrounding the reward system. Nevertheless, it must have brought a measure of comfort to the gangster to know that he could have direct dealings with the head of the CID while Albany's detectives were trying to lock him up.

But six months into Albany's investigations, in May 1981, Powis cancelled one of their meetings to discuss the Silver Bullion reward. Garner, who was planning to argue again for the full payment, was outraged and, at his behest, Lundy rushed to his typewriter and dashed off a long letter to Powis. Referring to Garner by his informant's code-name of 'Dave Granger', Lundy claimed that he had just left 'a very disappointed and irate informant'.

In the five pages that followed Lundy ranged from special

pleading for Garner to denying that the criminal was involved in crime. He also issued clear threats against the Yard about the damage they would suffer if they did not comply with Garner's demands. Lundy had to move fast; the previous day Harry Clement and his squad had raided Gibson's large house in Enfield and unearthed two compromising pictures of him with Garner and Ross.

The whole thrust of the letter was aimed at forcing Powis to back Garner and himself for the reward:

> I am a dedicated, hardworking officer and I have achieved outstanding successes in recent years in the war against major criminals. I think it right, Sir, that I should express in writing the feelings of 'Granger' and myself so that the situation can be clarified. There is no doubt that 'Granger' has achieved successes in the war against major criminals far in excess of any other informant, possibly in the history of the Metropolitan police.
>
> There are criminals serving thousands of years imprisonment due to information supplied by him . . . I think I should make it clear that I owe no allegiance to 'Granger' and he knows that I would arrest him if he participates or has participated in crime. He believes he is under investigation, as he has explained to yourself and DAC Steventon, but has never asked me to interfere in any way.
>
> However, he states that allegations which he believes are under investigation are malicious allegations by supergrasses who suspect him of being a grass. I do not discuss such matters with him, indeed he does not ask me to do so, but did speak to yourself having sought an interview.

This was an amazing revelation. Lundy was confirming that Garner knew about Operation Albany, that the gangster had discussed the allegations with the two joint heads of the Yard's CID, Powis and Steventon, and that Lundy himself had gone behind the back of Clement and made his own representations on Garner's behalf. No other criminal could expect such special treatment.

Lundy then raised the unpleasant fact that his own career had taken a nasty swerve after the Silver Bullion inquiry.

> Whilst awaiting promotion to Detective Superintendent I was suddenly transferred to 'J' District as Detective Chief Inspector. Such a move was unprecedented on the Flying Squad when a senior officer was awaiting promotion. For some time 'many tongues wagged' but I continued to work hard, with clear conscience, but rather puzzled and disappointed.

After this less than searing self-appraisal Lundy returned to the Silver Bullion reward and issued a direct threat to his Deputy Assistant Commissioner.

> As you know he has instructed solicitors in a claim against the assessors . . . in view of the context of the interviews about that matter with all interested parties, it would appear that considerable embarrassment will be caused if we are called to a civil court action. 'Granger' has not asked that the assessors should be told to pay the full amount of the reward but has asked that 'police' should not restrict their decision as to the amount but should leave it to them to so decide.

The threat dealt with, Lundy then returned to his stilted but grovelling style.

> I hope one day, Sir, to be promoted to your rank and sit in your seat . . . I assure you my devotion to this job and the fight against crime continues wholeheartedly and respectfully in spite of the foregoing and other disappointments.

When the letter was leaked to the *Guardian* in October 1985, the Yard refused to comment. Operation Albany's Harry Clement, by then in retirement, did. He made his feelings known and said that Lundy's approach to Powis was 'improper and unethical'. Clement added that he was 'outraged' that an officer junior to him had made representations over his head about the subject of his own investigations.

The hero of the Silver Bullion Robbery was undoubtedly Tony Lundy. By 3 June 1980 he had recovered virtually all the stolen property and obtained confessions from the gang leaders. Yet 53 days later he was bundled off the elite Flying Squad to the Met's gulag, a divisional posting at Chingford in North-East London.

The move was made on the instructions of DAC Powis, who declined to give Lundy any explanation.

The catalyst was Lundy's curious relationship with Roy Garner. Although another six months were to pass before Moriarty began his disclosures, it must have dawned on DAC Powis that all was not well with the relationship between the gangster and the detective. The clues were near to hand, in fact they lay in three dockets on the Head of Detectives' desk. When he returned from a brief holiday on Monday 21 July 1980, Powis realised that 'Something Had To Be Done'.

Each docket contained an application for a reward payment. In each case the informant was Roy Garner, the officer backing him was Tony Lundy and the reward claimed was 10 per cent of the sum involved in three robberies. The first had been an armed hold-up of a Brinks-Mat security van carrying £40,000 in Rosslyn Hill, Hampstead, on 4 December 1979. That one seemed fairly straightforward and Garner would benefit by £4,000.

The second reward was more worrying. Earlier, in February 1980, two hard-up Hatton Garden jewellers had staged a bogus armed robbery in which £750,000 worth of gems had apparently disappeared. They submitted a fraudulent insurance claim but, with Garner's alleged involvement, the jewels were recovered and both men confessed. But there were question marks hanging over the way Lundy had conducted the investigation, and concern about the size of the reward claimed, a massive £75,000.

The third docket contained the documents relating to Garner's claim for the record £300,000 reward for supplying the information which solved the Silver Bullion Robbery.

Action was taken quickly against Lundy and Garner. Powis sent for the detective, complimented him on his recent successes and told him that when his promotion to Superintendent came through he would be posted to lecture at the Detective Training School at Hendon. But as soon as Lundy had left the room orders were issued for him to be ousted from the Flying Squad and posted to Chingford. The following Monday, 28 July 1980, Lundy was shocked to find himself making the long journey to the suburbs and the pleasures of investigating routine crime.

Having dealt with Lundy, Powis then sought out the loss adjusters who had been appointed to settle the Silver Bullion reward on behalf of the insurers. He met them in their office at the end of that week and pitched straight in with his opinion that 'Granger' did not deserve the full 10 per cent reward. Gervaise had already been in custody, said Powis, and it was only after lengthy interrogations of the suspects and further inquiries that their involvement was established and the silver recovered.

This does not square with Lundy's version of the investigation. According to his records Gervaise capitulated in 90 seconds and Gibson in slightly less. The silver was recovered within seven hours of Gibson's arrest. Clearly Powis was prepared to disregard this in order to cut Garner's claim down to size.

There had always been worries about the size of rewards and suspicions that they were often divided up between dishonest detectives and spurious informants. At intervals the Yard circulated new orders, tightening up the way rewards were claimed and paid. Just as regularly, corrupt detectives found ways round them and continued cutting up the proceeds. Powis set out to tackle this in 1978 when he ordered that he must be present when sums in excess of £500 were paid to informants. In one of his favourite terms, 'the probity of the transaction had to be open to the most searching audit'.

Naturally, Powis shuddered at the thought of a gangster like Garner laying his hands on £300,000 and argued that £5,000 should be the maximum, but he was faced with dissent in his ranks. Lundy argued strongly that the informant was deserving of exceptional reward and his report was endorsed by Superintendent David Little and also by Mike Taylor, Acting Commander of the Flying Squad.

Powis stood firm against this pressure. While he knew an insurance company could pay what it wanted, he insisted that the Met would not be involved in any payment in excess of £5,000. In any case, the reward could not be paid until after the silver robbers were sentenced so Garner still had many months to plot with his advisors.

Powis held the line after Gibson and company were jailed in January 1981 and Garner was furious; he too could play hardball. He briefed a solicitor and threatened to sue the insurers for the full £300,000 reward. He warned that he would bring the detectives to court as witnesses. It could all be very embarrassing, as Lundy so thoughtfully pointed out in his letter to Powis.

In mid-January Garner's lawyers went to the Yard and both Lundy and Little made statements about Garner's role in recovering the silver. A month later the insurer's solicitors, the City firm of Clyde & Co., went to the Yard and told Powis that 'Granger' had turned down their offer of £75,000 and was still pushing for the maximum. Could Powis give them any assistance in holding 'Granger' at bay? Was 'Granger' a criminal?

All Powis would tell them was that 'Granger' was not involved in the robbery — the one piece of evidence that would debar him from the reward. But he did not mention that Lundy, Garner's handler, had been removed from the Flying Squad and was about to become the target of a massive corruption investigation. In the tortuous months of negotiations that were to follow, the question marks hanging over Lundy, the man who recommended 'Granger' for the reward, were never revealed to the loss adjusters or their solicitors.

Garner tried to step up the pressure on Powis. More criminals' names were put forward to convince Powis of his worth and help him get his money. He passed on information about cocaine smuggling and then revealed that the Barry Brothers were printing their own £5 notes. But Powis did not budge from the figure of £5,000. On 28 May 1981 Powis cancelled a meeting with Garner and Lundy hurried to his typewriter.

Four days after Lundy's letter dropped on Powis's desk it was followed by Operation Albany's interim report on the arsons and intimidation investigations. Clement's view of Garner's criminality might be said to differ radically from Lundy's. However by mid-June the loss adjusters had accepted that they were contractually bound to pay 'Granger' for his information. They needed Powis to identify 'Granger' to them, before they would hand over the cheque. On 30 June DACs Powis and Steventon met Tim Wardlow and Stewart McDonald from Clyde & Co.

At the last minute the lawyers asked if there was any more the Yard could tell them about the credibility of 'Granger'? Suddenly Powis and Steventon played their last card. They announced that they could not be certain that 'Granger' had not been involved in the crime after all! The two solicitors were flabbergasted. If there was any substance to this suggestion, then they need not pay a penny.

Unfortunately Powis and Steventon had no more to offer. Garner's strategy had paid off and the Met's £5,000 barrier simply collapsed. Powis agreed that in the circumstances it was better if he did not know how much was to be paid to Garner but, along with DAC Steventon, he agreed to make the identification.

Twenty-four hours later, on Wednesday 1 July 1981, Powis and Steventon walked briskly round the corner from the Yard to Tothill Street, where Garner was waiting in a car with one of his several lawyers and one from Clyde & Co. They identified Garner and walked away. He was then given a cheque for £178,000, a discount having been negotiated for a quick settlement. Garner had won again.

Garner was still celebrating a week after pocketing the record reward cheque. So much so that he was stopped late at night near the Haymarket in his gold Mercedes by a young constable and invited to take a breath test. When he refused Garner was arrested and taken to Bow Street. His young woman companion went along too. At the police station he asked to make a phone call and then, to the astonishment of the night shift, roused a senior Yard officer from his bed.

'Hallo, it's Roy,' he announced, 'tell this lot to let me go, I won't be able to do that job for you.' Garner passed the phone to a uniform officer, who was told, 'There must be some mistake, this man does not drink and drive, let him go.' The uniform officer demurred and Garner was placed in a cell.

The police surgeon was called and Garner agreed to a blood test. The result showed him below the limit for a prosecution. He could have been prosecuted for failing to give a sample when first requested. This did not happen. The next day, with the blessing of the Yard, Garner flew to Toronto to buy more horses and stash more money in his secret Canadian account.

10 · GOD'S OWN TRUTH

THE COUNTRY COPPERS came for Billy Young at eight in the morning. He had turned his back on crime and was trying to build up a newsagent's business at Forest Gate in East London. The visit was quite unlike a Flying Squad raid. They did not smash the door down before dawn and they did not drag him away. The detective in charge said, politely, 'I'm arresting you in connection with armed robberies and burglaries — but you can finish marking up the papers first.'

Country detectives from Number 5 Regional Crime Squad were not soft. They had discovered that if they treated these top London robbers with impeccable courtesy and made it clear that they were totally incorruptible, they usually got excellent results.

The most successful drive against the armed robbers was run not from the Yard but from a police station further up the Thames at Reading. 'Operation Carter' was set up by Number 5 Regional Crime Squad. They based their campaign on the evidence of five supergrasses and succeeded in jailing dozens of major criminals.

Carter grew out of the capture of a London robbery team that had taken £34,000 from a security van at Hemel Hempstead in 1977. Some of the team turned supergrass and the names started to pour out. By June 1980 5RCS had got round to lifting Fred

Sinfield, who had been active with all the best robbery teams for a decade. This time, there was no chance of acquittal and he too asked for a supergrass deal.

Sinfield talked a little about Tony Lundy but, most important of all, he incriminated the bulky figure of Billy Young, a prolific robber and burglar. Young decided to become Carter's fifth supergrass. He had a lot of information which was to engage not just 5RCS but also the interest of two separate teams of Yard detectives.

The Carter supergrasses ran simultaneously with Lundy's 'Factory' at Finchley. All the criminals were Londoners, most of them knew each other very well, and it was chance whether they were captured by the Met or by 5RCS — but there the similarities ended. Their confessions appear to have been written on different planets. Lundy's grasses could reel off the names of criminals but were quite ignorant of police corruption. But the criminals singing their hearts out at Reading admitted that they had kept their freedom in the past only by paying vast amounts to London detectives. Billy Young produced a further tranche of corruption stories about criminals and corrupt detectives when he took 5RCS's deal.

The professional criminals who worked with Young share the opinion of the detectives who handled him. They admit, bitterly, 'Billy Young told God's own truth.' Harry Clement, who debriefed Young in London adds, 'He was a witness of truth.' Former Detective Superintendent Tony Hill of the Hertfordshire police and 5RCS remembers that Young was always careful to distinguish between his first-hand experiences and what he had learned on the criminal grapevine. So when Young went 'super' many criminals and corrupt policemen trembled.

Operation Albany was just up and running in London when Young opted for the deal offered by the provincial detectives in the late autumn of 1980. Number 5 RCS took down his amazing confessions in police stations across the Home Counties but Young's statements were not officially handed over to the Met until well into 1981. Unofficially, Young's allegations triggered a series of confidential phone calls. Number 5 RCS tipped off trustworthy detectives in the Met about what Young was revealing. In the other direction, a senior Met officer, with much to fear from Young, phoned the Regional Crime Squad and warned that Young was not be believed. That in turn was passed back to honest officers at the Yard.

Billy Young's was not a headline name but he was well respected among first-division robbers. As Clement comments, 'He had worked with men who were daily names in Scotland Yard, he had worked with the cream.' He had been to prison but not as often as such an active criminal would have expected. The reason was obvious: he paid bribes. He also paid money to detectives when they tipped him off about jobs worth doing, and when the job came off, their 'whack' would be handed over.

Young moved in the same world as Garner and Lundy and their friend Lennie Gibson. He became part of the North London pub circuit, rubbing shoulders with this bizarre group of major criminals and senior detectives. He first met Garner, Ross and Gibson in The Horns pub in the late 1960s. Young had just come out of prison and was looking for somewhere to live. Ross rented him a flat, and from his landlord's gossip Young realised that Garner and Ross were active robbers. They promised that he would soon be taken on a good armed robbery.

A few months later Young learned from Gibson that Garner and Ross had left him off the hijack of the KLM bullion van, so he 'grassed' it to a detective sergeant. But nothing happened, and in September 1972 he was invited by Garner to join the raid on the bankers Brown, Shipley. Young later told his captors about these and other robberies; some of them involved both Garner and his friends in the police.

If 5RCS had investigated all Young's allegations there might have been a very different result, but their bosses begrudged the budget and argued that it was not up to them to investigate corruption in the Met. Months passed while the Home Counties policemen investigated the allegations Young made against his fellow criminals. As in the past the delay gave the corrupt detectives in London time to build their defences against the coming onslaught.

The 5RCS investigation was not conducted entirely without help from the Met. They were more than happy to borrow officers recommended by Harry Clement, for whom there was a compliment from Billy Young. Initially he had insisted to his captors at 5RCS that he was not prepared to be seen alone by detectives from the Met. But once he had met Clement and his team Young told 5RCS that he was so impressed by their honesty and dedication that he had changed his mind and was quite prepared to go on being interviewed by them without his provincial minders.

When the Met formally received Young's allegations they split them into two sections. The information about the criminals was passed to Operation Albany. Young blew apart the claim made by Gibson and Lundy at the Old Bailey six months earlier that the Silver Bullion robber had gone straight for ten years and that the robbery was some kind of aberration. Young recalled that Gibson had planned at least 42 robberies over the previous decade. Many were aimed at security vans. Out of the 42 jobs, 15 were aborted before the day, 10 failed, but 17 times he escaped with cash, bullion or jewels. Far from going straight for the last ten years, as Lundy had allowed the Old Bailey to think, Gibson had even been on an armed robbery in Tottenham with Billy Young a mere month before the Silver Bullion job.

When Gibson was not abroad with his sawn-off, Young recalls that he would pester other criminals in The Eagle, asking if anyone knew of a good 'tie-up' burglary worth doing in a private house. Dolph Aguda had been almost as prolific. He had set out to do at least 33 robberies and 11 had been successful. His nephew Ron Aguda had been allowed to take part in five, two of which brought home the goods.

Harry Clement was only able to investigate a handful of Young's claims. Most of the robberies lacked sufficient corroboration to put before a jury and the DPP ruled that any offence over five years old had to be ignored. However, he did convict the Barry Brothers, who had been on the Tottenham robbery with Young and Gibson just before the Silver Bullion job.

Detective Chief Superintendent Alan Stagg did not enjoy his last assignment before retiring. Young's allegations against Scotland Yard detectives were given to him and he set up his own investigation team, which reported to Deputy Assistant Commissioner Ron Steventon. It became known as the Stagg/Steventon inquiry. Eventually he submitted his massive report and, with great relief, left the Met. Stagg had been given the unenviable task of investigating corruption allegations against the Flying Squad's highest flyer, Tony Lundy, newly promoted to Detective Superintendent.

The investigation was triggered by an anonymous letter which had all the hallmarks of coming from a police source. It alleged that Tony Lundy and other officers had stolen the 12 missing ingots from the Silver Bullion robbery. The letter brought to a head a number of rumours that had been circulating since June the previous year, when the bulk of the silver was recovered from Gibson's lock-up.

What disturbed the Stagg team was the mystery of the Aguda key. When Dolph Aguda had been arrested he had in his pocket a key to the lock-up and it was taken from him with the rest of his property. Why had he not mentioned it when he and Gibson confessed? Why did the officers, led by Lundy, who went to the lock-up to find the silver, have to force the door?

And where was the rest of the robbery gear; shotguns, masks and police uniforms that Gibson customarily stored in the garage? Their discovery would have damaged Gibson's claim that he had not been involved in crime for a decade. Could the key have been smuggled out of the police station following Gibson's private confession to Lundy? Had a bent detective gone to the lock-up and removed a car boot full of silver ingots along with that compromising robbery equipment?

Other rumours identified a scrap metal dealer known to Garner who was said to have been asked by a detective on the Robbery Squad to melt down the bars for him. While these stories fed the Yard gossip machine, Lundy insisted that Mickey Sewell, now conveniently absent, had taken the ingots when he disappeared.

News of the internal investigation was leaked to the *News of the World*, which revealed:

> startling allegations of police corruption involving one of Britain's biggest robberies. Several high-ranking officers are said to have cashed in when armed high-jackers snatched £3.5 million in silver bullion.
>
> Most of the load was recovered but now an informer has told the Yard: a detective provided uniforms so the gang could pose as policemen to stop the lorry at a bogus checkpoint. Two officers stole 12 of the ingots, worth £144,000.

Lundy was repeatedly questioned by Stagg's team but absolutely no evidence was found to back up the allegation. The Yard has still never explained why the detectives needed to break open the door to Gibson's lock-up when they had a key in their possession.

There was so much that seemed wrong about the Silver Bullion investigation. The *News of the World* story disclosed another strand of the Stagg inquiry. It continued:

> A detective told an informer where the bullion was hidden and ordered him to claim the reward. This was later shared with a senior officer. The allegations are being investigated by the Yard's anti-corruption squad, CIB2.

The Stagg team climbed all over the Silver Bullion inquiry, particularly Lundy's private interview with Gibson and Aguda. They took the view that it was utterly wrong for the three to have been left alone for hours without a police witness to Lundy's version of what was said. One member of the Stagg team described Lundy's record of that evening as 'pure make-believe'.

What troubled them most was the nature of the relationship between Lundy and Garner. Was information passed from Garner the informant to Lundy the detective — or was it the other way around? Had Gervaise's disclosures about the bullion robbery team been obtained slightly earlier and then, to get the vast reward, submitted in Garner's name? The Stagg team visited Dolph Aguda in prison but the DPP would not accept statements from a convicted robber against London policemen so he refused to sign them and went on serving his sentence.

Inevitably, the investigators turned to look at the other huge reward, £37,500, that Powis had paid to Garner in 1980. The crime itself was unremarkable by Hatton Garden standards. Jeweller Wilf Hogg had claimed that he was ambushed by armed robbers early one morning in the Garden, a month before the Silver Bullion Robbery. Hogg had a convincing story: he was found tied up in a van a mile away, minus a collection of jewels worth £750,000 that he was taking to sell in Saudi Arabia.

He and his partner John Heath lodged an insurance claim, the insurers offered a £75,000 reward and the Flying Squad sought the robbers. Eventually the jewellers confessed to setting up a bogus ambush and making a false insurance claim. The jewels were recovered and the £75,000 reward was paid out. On Lundy's recommendation half went to Roy Garner. The rest was paid to an informant in Sussex who went under the pseudonym of 'Sean Murphy'.

When the Stagg team examined the records of the Heath and Hogg investigation they discovered a curious sequence of events. 'Sean Murphy' was in prison at the time of the bogus robbery and his information about it was brought to the Yard by a detective from the Sussex police. Immediately afterwards Garner was credited with supplying similar information. The Sussex police were surprised when they learned that their informant was not to receive the full payment. They could not see any reason to divide the reward in half.

This incident was a turning point for the Stagg team. Their suspicions had already been raised when Garner was given the credit for providing the crucial information about the Silver Bullion Robbery. The Hatton Garden investigation only fuelled the fear that criminal intelligence was flowing out of the Yard, not into it.

Every fortnight Detective Superintendent Colin MacDonald travelled to Cardiff prison with Detective Sergeant David Valentine to interview Billy Young. He was in standard supergrass isolation in a small suite of cells where he cooked his meals, watched TV and pressed weights.

Young's memory ranged back over his years with the North London Circus and he recalled a story told him one night by an angry Stevie Salter. In the mid-1970s, said Salter, he had supplied Lundy with a free lorryload of wooden fencing for his house in Cowley Hill Road. This was in addition to the money Salter claimed he had paid out to Garner and others after the collapse of the long firm fraud with the drinks warehouse. Salter said he had had enough of being conned and had made a statement which was locked away in his solicitor's office.

Young told MacDonald, 'I was at this time active in crime and could not afford to fall out with Lundy and Spicer, so I told Spicer of the existence of the statement. Spicer said he would frighten the life out of Salter and tell him the police suspected him for all sorts of things. Spicer told me that he had been told by Lundy to leave it and do not upset Salter.'

One night soon afterwards, some of the Circus were drinking at Salter's farmhouse in Cuffley. Lundy's bookmaker friend Spicer was drunk and Billy Young feared that he would disclose his knowledge of the statement to Salter. Young tried to change the subject. 'There was an argument and eventually a fight. I remember saying I would nick him and his mate Tony Lundy.' Six years later Young did just that but the Stagg team could not persuade Salter, who was heavily involved in a number of criminal enterprises with Garner, to talk to them. Nevertheless the story of the fencing would come back to haunt Lundy.

What made Billy so bitter was having to pay money to avoid being fitted up for crimes he had not done. This was extortion. One such incident, he complained angrily to 5RCS, followed an armed robbery at Murphy's civil engineering contractors' offices in Highbury. Young had not been involved.

A detective sergeant from Brixton had accused Young of being on the Murphy robbery and wanted £1,000 to leave him out of it. Young reluctantly agreed to pay the money, was interviewed in the presence of his solicitor and then handed a middleman £1,000. Young named this officer as well as another who allegedly extorted £3,600 to leave his name out of another robbery which Young again knew nothing about.

David Spicer was a pivotal member of the North London Circus. The allegations were that he was both the cutout for corrupt payments to detectives and prolific in suggesting houses to be burgled.

There was a powerful confrontation, hosted by 5RCS, when Young was brought to identify Spicer as the man he had named. Spicer queried why Young was revealing so much and Young riposted:

'You frightened me to death, Dave. You knew I would have to pay although I had fuck all to do with Murphy's. You knew that if I got nicked and the Old Bill came steaming into my place it would have destroyed Gail and everything. They were real bad things that you were doing Dave and you know it.'

Young's allegations were made public in May 1982 at Snaresbrook Crown Court, on the north-east border of London and Essex. There were six defendants in the dock. One of them was Spicer, who was accused of conspiracy to burgle. The charge was spelled out in court as 'sticking up' names of potential victims, many of whom were his acquaintances.

Number 5 RCS had swooped on Spicer at his Finchley home at 5am on Friday 6 March 1981. When cautioned, Spicer spoke volumes in one sentence. 'I know what this is. It's Billy Young.'

Spicer denied all Young's accusations when he came to trial. During cross-examination he claimed that, while watching Arsenal at Highbury one day, he had bumped into Kenny Ross, Garner's partner. Ross told him that Young had been arrested and said, 'You will be one of the first to go.' Spicer told the court he had seen Garner and Ross with Lundy at boxing matches and at The Torrington Arms. 'Kenny and Roy would be together with all of us, including Lundy.

'Roy Garner was more a friend of mine than Kenny Ross. I was introduced to him by Gibson, who used to drink in The Torrington when Lundy was there. One night Gibson and Young were taking the mickey out of Lundy. He lost his temper and said he would nick the pair of them. I was quite friendly with Mr Lundy — me and Lennie Gibson. Both Lennie and Mr Lundy trusted me. I have known Tony Lundy for 15 years.'

The jury, however, did not believe Spicer and the judge jailed him for three years, fined him £10,000 and described him as 'a viper who has sunk about as low as man can'. Three other burglars were jailed on Young's testimony. All the police officers named by Young have denied his allegations. The Appeal Court later criticised the judge's handling of Spicer's case and quashed his conviction. Obviously he had not had a fair trial. He now runs a fruit stall in Barnet market.

The probe into Lundy commenced in the spring of 1981. There was a conference between Clement and Stagg but it was December before a high-level meeting was called at the DPP's office. Deputy Director Kenneth Dowling was in the chair and two other officials were present. Both Stagg and Clement attended. Their purpose was to corroborate the corruption allegations against Lundy with any information Operation Albany might have. There was a slight element of farce about this meeting because Albany had been closed down by the Yard a month earlier.

11 · THE TIME BOMB

BILLY YOUNG'S GREATEST criminal coup went further than just holding up security trucks at gunpoint; he achieved every robber's dream. Young cast around for a malleable detective, corrupted him, enriched him and finally destroyed him.

Young's victim was Detective Sergeant Tommy Miller who had come down from Scotland to join the Met in May 1967. He was promoted to detective work on divisional squads but never achieved his ambition to join the Flying Squad. That ambition became his downfall. Miller assumed the way to acceptance by the Squad was by associating with criminals and doing them favours. He hoped this might bring back a flow of information that would gain him kudos with his bosses. Instead, he was captured by the criminals and became one himself.

Billy Young had met Miller in The Eagle, Garner's den of thieves. It was 1973 and Garner and Ross made the introduction, privately assuring Young that Miller was 'all right'. Miller was so 'all right' that for £50 he would 'borrow' criminal intelligence files from the Yard. He did it for Garner and Ross and he did it for Gibson. It was very valuable for these active robbers to find out how much the police knew about them. The secret files might also give clues about who was grassing on them.

Young spent many a night drinking after hours in The Eagle with Miller, trying to persuade him to suggest places worth robbing. Young said to him, 'If you get to hear about anything such as stolen property in somebody's lock-up, tell me first before you blokes get there. Then I can clear it out.' If Young is to be believed, Detective Miller became a steady flow of information, suggestions and even provided equipment to help with robberies.

Young recalled, 'On one ocasion he asked me if I could do with a couple of police uniforms with hats and I said they could come in handy some time. I said they would have to be a large size, taking into account that myself and Gibson would use them, and as a result of this he passed over two uniforms. He did not ask for payment and none was offered. These uniforms were passed on to Gibson to be put in the Arnos Grove lock-up.' One of these uniforms was worn by Mickey Gervaise when ambushing the silver bullion lorry.

At another of their regular meetings Miller offered the name and address of a diamond dealer in Finchley who was worth robbing. Young took the proposition to Gibson and Dolph Aguda. 'We decided that we would use the police uniforms that Miller had got us a couple of years before and that we would have to con the diamond dealer as if we used violence we would have Lundy and his robbery squad at Finchley, which was only about a mile away, breathing down our necks either to "nick" us or "blag" us for a share.' They wore the uniforms and used a search warrant supplied by Miller. But when they tried to bluff their way into the house, the occupiers were unimpressed and the 'policemen' backed out saying they must have got the wrong address. Years later, the occupiers confirmed the bizarre visit.

Another job suggested by Miller was started just before Christmas 1978. He had learned of a West London flat with a safe containing 600 Krugerrands and some melted gold. Miller even took Young for a ride, to see the target building. 'We drove down to Elgin Avenue in a red CID car. I think it was a Hillman and it definitely had a police radio in it. We drove into Elgin Avenue from the Harrow Road direction and Miller pointed out a block of flats.'

Young, Gibson and Aguda started their observations but they were interrupted when Gibson took his girlfriend off on holiday to Las Palmas in January 1979. Eventually they fell out about how to pull the job. Young reported back to Detective Miller. 'During this time I had been on other work and had my usual meets with Miller. On several of these meets he had asked me how this job was getting on and finally I told him that it was definitely off.'

The most lucrative job that Miller put Billy Young's way came in 1974. One of Miller's colleagues had discovered that an Indian businessman, Mr Mohammed Ali, kept huge sums of money in his home. Miller got his police colleague drunk, looked in his notebook and found Mr Ali's phone number. He passed it to Young, gave him a blank search warrant and suggested that he recruit another criminal and, posing as police officers, 'do the place'.

Young turned to Garner's muscleman at The Eagle, Johnny Brixton, who said that he knew two suitable people to join them. Young enquired, 'Do these people look like Old Bill?' Brixton replied, 'They look more like Old Bill than Old Bill.' The pair he had in mind were Garner and Ross. Bearing in mind Garner's double role in the world of crime, the remark had more than passing irony.

But Brixton dragged his heels and one night in The Eagle an irritated Billy Young confided the information to Gibson, who decided to get to work immediately. The first problem was fitting an address to Mr Ali's phone number. 'Don't worry about that,' said Gibson, 'I'll get it, leave it to me.' Gibson then went to a contact who approached his friend Tony Lundy, claiming that he was having some problems with a bad debtor. He had got the man's telephone number but he needed an address; could Tony use police channels to help?

There is no doubt that Lundy was taken in by this story. Allegedly he made the usual application to the Yard's C1 department, where such traces were done, and in due course came back with the news that the house was in Salmon Street, Wembley. The night of the robbery Brixton came armed with a PPK handgun. Brixton, Gibson and Young all dressed smartly and wore trilbys, to look like detectives. Young even dyed his hair; 'up to the line of where the hat would sit on my hair I sprayed silver spray. I'd seen Roy Garner do this on one occasion.' They went up the drive, past Mr Ali's Rolls-Royce with its MAL 1 numberplate, knocked on the door and Brixton announced that they were police officers searching for counterfeit currency.

He produced the genuine search warrant and asked if there was any money in the house. Mr Ali's wife, Margaret, produced a carrier bag full of cash from a safe and Brixton sat at a table, pretending to examine it. Young then asked, 'Have you any more money on the premises?' and Mr Ali trustingly replied, 'Yes, I have got money on the premises, I am a very rich man,' and told his son, 'Get the money.' A heavy box of banknotes was produced and the robbers were silent for a moment, unable to believe their luck. Young took the initiative, drew the gun from Brixton's pocket, and ordered the family to the floor. In their hurry to leave with the box they forgot to take the carrier bag full of notes. Back at Young's flat, in a Gibson-owned house in Firs Avenue, Muswell Hill, they counted the cash and it came to £64,000. Young remembers that it was shared three ways after putting aside £6,000 for Miller. He also alleged that there was a further payout.

Later in court, Billy Young recalled a conversation with 'big-hearted' Gibson about Lundy being given £1,000 for his trouble. 'I know this money was given to Lundy and I'm sure Gibson paid it out himself.'

Young's allegations continued. 'Within a couple of days Gibson tells me that the contact called him down to his shop and said that Lundy was doing his nut over the phone number and the address. Lundy had said that if he'd known what it was to be, he could have got it some other way. After Lundy is supposed to have done his nut Gibson tells me that Ross and Garner have been in touch with him and there was a meet laid on for that evening.

'Gibson picked me up and we drove to the meet and sitting in a car was Ross and Brixton. We parked and both walked back and got in the motor. Then Garner walked up from his turning and got in. Ross had begun to tell us that "X" [a very senior Scotland Yard officer] had been to Ross and Garner and accused them of the Indian job.

'Garner stated that "X" wanted £25,000 at first and that he had got him down to £20,000. He said that "X" had said to Kenny Ross that this was his method of operation and that they were going to be put on ID parades for the Indian and Ross had turned round and said they'd go on the parades if they were straight. He said "X" said he couldn't guarantee that.

'We realised that we were being blagged but there was nothing we could do about it. At this point Brixton said, "In that case I had better put my money towards it." As a result of this Brixton, Gibson and myself had to put in £6,666 each.'

The Stagg team examined Young's claims carefully. The first thing they went looking for was corroboration of his claim that Lundy had obtained an address to go with the phone number. At the time of the robbery Lundy was lecturing at D9, the Met's detective training school at Hendon.

The records of all requests from detectives for traces of addresses and phone numbers were stored in the C1 department. Alan Stagg had worked there previously and he knew exactly what he was looking for. If the request existed it would be in what the Yard called a 'Book 40', a miscellaneous ledger. Without giving any warning Stagg turned up at the C1 office, found the book and took it.

There it was, absolutely clear: the entry in the ledger gave the details of Lundy's request and the fact that he was then stationed at D9. Surely this was corroboration of Young's allegation.

A few days later Stagg went to see DAC Halsey, who supervised the investigation in its initial stages. Stagg outlined Young's allegations while keeping the C1 ledger, literally, behind his back. Halsey summed up by saying, 'It would be a good piece of evidence if we could substantiate Lundy's part in it.' Stagg then produced the ledger. Stagg's team had considerable respect for Halsey and he agreed to forward their request that Lundy's and Garner's phones should be put under surveillance. This was refused at another level of the Yard and any suggestion that Lundy should be suspended was dismissed as unthinkable.

Next the investigators looked for corroboration of Young's allegations that money had been paid to Detective Sergeant Miller. The supergrass said that Miller had put his £6,000 from the Salmon Street robbery into a building society account and then spent £2,000 on a set of chairs and a table from Harrods and another £1,000 on a new fitted kitchen. The Stagg team traced the building society account and even a cashier who remembered Miller paying the money in, still in its bank wrappers. Then they went to Miller's house — and there was the Harrods furniture and the new kitchen.

Miller of course had an explanation. The £6,000 was money he had saved while living cheaply in a police section house. His claim was backed up by a former Met detective who had left well before he qualified for a full pension. Miller could not remember anything about bank wrappers on his savings.

The Senior officer 'X', whose name we have deleted, had left the Yard and there was no other way that evidence could be found to corroborate Young's allegation.

Detective Inspector Peter Walsh never made any secret of his hatred of corruption. He was forthright, to the point of professional suicide, in walking up to senior officers in pubs and denouncing them as 'bent bastards'. Walsh was based at Wembley and was given the investigation into the robbery of Mr Ali at Salmon Street.

He soon learned that the robbers had produced a genuine search warrant to get into the house and feedback from his own informants suggested police involvement. Before long senior officers were telling him to drop his inquiries. He ignored their 'advice' and for his pains was assaulted one night in the Flying Squad office at the Yard by Detective Chief Inspector Alec Eist, who sought to provoke a breach of discipline by Walsh.

The key to blowing the whole business wide open was to get the robbers on an identification parade. They had not worn masks and with luck the Ali family should pick them out. The crime would carry a long sentence and the names of their bent police friends might well be offered in exchange for leniency. Walsh pressed on and then, to his amazement, was taken off active investigations and moved to a desk job.

Determined to find the criminals, he went to a meeting one Sunday, in his own time, with an informant who held out the promise that he knew the robbers' names. Unexpectedly, another man turned up who was on bail and awaiting trial. It was a breach of Met rules to meet with anybody on bail without a senior officer's consent. Walsh was obviously being set up and before long a complaint went into the Yard that he had taken a £2,000 bribe.

He was suspended for two years, investigated and finally cleared. Walsh was interviewed by a panel of psychiatrists who found nothing wrong with him and asked, in tones of commiseration, if he had seen the film *Serpico*, about a New York policeman who singlehandedly took on corruption. In August 1976, without ever returning to duty, Walsh was discharged as medically unfit for police service. He has never been told what those medical grounds were.

Walsh left the force, in his own words, 'totally shattered and disillusioned'. Just before he resigned his wife went to see a senior Yard officer who told her, 'The trouble with Peter is that he is too honest.' Walsh remained frustrated and puzzled at this inglorious end to his dedicated police work. A decade later we gave him copies of the confessions of supergrass Billy Young. Walsh confirmed to us that Young's description of the robbery matched exactly what the Ali family had told him.

Keith Bryson had been in Tony Lundy's bedroom and wanted to tell the world what he had found. The venue he chose was Willesden Crown Court in January 1983 and in the dock was Bryson's friend Keith Brown, accused of conspiracy to rob. Two Robbery Squad officers alleged they had found 'robbery paraphernalia' in his West London house and that he had made verbal admissions of his intention to rob a security van. Brown denied this and counter-claimed that he had been fitted up because the previous year he had done a favour for Bryson.

Bryson duly took the oath and revealed that he was a professional burglar who had been caught redhanded in Lundy's Cowley Hill house. He claimed that he had found an attaché case stuffed full of pesetas and US dollars as well as Georgian silver and valuable stamp albums. Bryson added that the police who arrested him said he had stolen property worth £47,000 but on the charge sheet, to his amazement and considerable gratification, the value of the property was reduced to just £3,670.

Bryson, a raffish character, continued: 'When I was charged I thought, "Cor, that's a result," but I kept quiet.' He was delighted at only getting a 12-month sentence. To round off his evidence Bryson added: 'Lundy is Lundy . . . you don't compare him with anyone. He's him. He ain't half fitted some people up. He's the main reason for Keith Brown sitting there.'

Brown's defence case was that Robbery Squad officers had fitted him up for having the audacity to help Bryson with bail sureties after he had been charged with the Lundy burglary. Brown claimed he was warned that for this undiplomatic act he would soon be joining Bryson in prison.

Lundy came to court and, having denied Bryson's claims about his personal wealth, announced: 'I have dealt with and was responsible for the arrest of more major criminals than probably anyone in the history of the Metropolitan Police. I have dealt with hundreds of the top echelon of criminals and crimes involving millions of pounds throughout the whole country.

'I have been subjected to a prolonged, continuing and malicious attack from numerous criminals and their associates backed up on many occasions by certain representatives of the media.' The jury took just 55 minutes to acquit Keith Brown. Stagg's team then interviewed Bryson at great length.

It all came to nothing. After three years Stagg's inquiries were at an end. The DPP refused to prosecute any detective on the word of supergrass Billy Young, although his evidence was believed by juries when he was called against other common criminals.

In August 1983, before the Yard sent the bulky file off to the archives, Deputy Assistant Commissioner Ron Steventon added a two-page memo. Any policeman aware of Steventon's experience with the Porn Squad and other corruption inquiries should have paid attention to the message contained within it. The memo was buried in the Yard archives but, like a time bomb, it lay there ticking away.

Steventon began by summarising what the Yard knew about Roy Garner and Kenny Ross: they were 'in the forefront of major crime and are dubbed by a number of leading criminals as "Mr Fixits" and intermediaries between Police and the criminal fraternity'. Garner was Lundy's informant and had received six substantial rewards in the previous five years. Garner had been nominated by Lundy for the Heath and Hogg bogus Hatton Garden robbery reward and also for the Silver Bullion reward. So far, the memo was a statement of fact. Steventon's next comment was explosive.

'Some evidence has been deduced in respect of both these cases which suggests that Garner was not the informant he was claimed to be and that he was merely exploiting information he had received from Lundy.' In one sentence, Steventon had turned on its head the belief of the Yard leadership that high-grade criminal intelligence was coming from Garner, through Lundy, to them. Steventon's thesis was clear: valuable information appeared to be going in the reverse direction, from the Yard, through Lundy, to the criminal Garner. Steventon made no suggestions about where the reward money paid to Garner might be ending up.

Steventon's verdict should have been enough to end any detective's career overnight. Relentlessly the memo delivered further blows to Lundy's reputation. The compromising photographs of Lundy socialising with Garner and Gibson were noted, then Steventon went on to look at the reliability of supergrasses Billy Young and another criminal, Fred Sinfield, who had also made corruption allegations. The conclusion was damning again to Lundy: 'They have not been found to have told lies and Young has come up to proof in criminal trials.'

Steventon's next paragraph continued the demolition. 'Lundy has to all outward appearance been a successful operational detective and it is only when all the circumstances of his involvement with Garner are examined that grave doubts must be expressed as to his integrity. This view is reinforced by his failure to strictly comply with pocket book and diary regulations and his frequent resort to the excuse that he cannot remember events in detail on some issues which deserve a better explanation. On matters of little consequence he displays the clarity of recollection which is expected in an officer of his rank.'

Steventon was clear about what action should follow. 'I am of the opinion that the D. of P.P. will decline to institute criminal proceedings and the breaches of discipline revealed in relation to the pocket book and diary may be the only ways of dealing with Mr Lundy.' Then came the bombshell: 'I feel bound to express a personal opinion and regrettably there is a dearth of evidence to support it, but it is my belief that Lundy is a corrupt officer who has long exploited his association with Garner.' That was it; however qualified, Steventon had committed to paper the ultimate criticism of a fellow police officer. The word 'corrupt' jumped off the page. Finally Steventon made his recommendation. 'Consideration should be given to removing him from specialist duty.' That meant a swift transfer out of the CID and into uniform.

The memo went to Deputy Commissioner Albert Laugharne, an outsider who came from the Lancashire police straight to the number two job in the Met. He replied the next day: 'Thank you for your frankness and for the hard work you and your team of officers have put in on this. After your retirement I will arrange for your successor to handle this with the able help of Det. Chief Superintendent Stagg.' Laugharne did not know that Stagg was also about to retire and could not guess that he himself would soon be forced out on health grounds. But before Laugharne retired he wrote a forceful letter to the Police Complaints Board, the predecessor of the Complaints Authority. 'Lundy ought to have been above reproach. The handling of informants, especially in respect of the information he conveyed to Garner and the disregard of administrative directions in relation to the recording of interviews, leaves much to be desired. Indeed they are such as to cause concern in an officer of his rank.'

Laugharne ended with a disclosure: he told the Board that Lundy had been 'given advice'. Advice is the lowest level of discipline, but discipline it is and it would have been entered on Lundy's record. He had been investigated and his character was now officially and permanently blemished.

The Yard's response to Steventon and Laugharne was predictable: it hid the documents away and remained silent when Lundy declared in public that he had been completely exonerated. There was good reason for the Yard to bury its head in the sand. If it got out that a detective who had put so many men in jail had been labelled 'corrupt' by the Yard, the Appeal Court could be besieged for years.

No Appeal judge, on learning that police records presented in the original trials were suspect, could allow the convictions to stand. Every man jailed on Lundy's evidence would point to Laugharne's comment 'the disregard of administrative directions in relation to the recording of interviews leaves much to be desired' and argue that confessions they had always denied making could now no longer be admissible. The same would go for any statements Lundy had taken. The vast swathes of uncorroborated allegations from Lundy's supergrasses would be eliminated. This was confirmed to us by a senior Yard officer with close knowledge of the Stagg inquiry.

Nobody realised this better than Lundy, who when under pressure in the future would announce, 'I have no doubt that numerous criminals backed up by certain sections of the media are determined to discredit me and thus open the floodgates from prison.' It might sound gibberish to the public but the code was heard loud and clear at the Yard: 'If you do not protect me, you will suffer disgrace and embarrassment.'

To the outside world Lundy had been vindicated. The Yard went along with this fiction. In the summer of 1984 Lundy was awarded a Good Conduct medal and the following year a board, chaired by Assistant Commissioner John Dellow, selected him for promotion to the rank of Detective Chief Superintendent.

Detective Sergeant Tommy Miller was not so fortunate. One of the Stagg team commented, 'Miller was a loner. He didn't have any protection at the Yard.' Later, Miller was to contact the *Observer* with the advice 'You don't know the half of what was going on . . . ' and said that he might be prepared to meet reporters when he returned from a holiday. But he never called again.

Retired Detective Chief Superintendent Harry Clement recalls that as the pressure mounted on Miller he made an approach, through a colleague, asking about the possibility of going supergrass. This would have been remarkable; Miller would have been the first ever police supergrass. Clement passed back the message that Miller would have to tell absolutely everything he knew. He heard no more.

Miller was suspended for two years and in May 1983 was served with four internal discipline charges. At the beginning of 1984 he was allowed to retire on an enhanced medical pension without ever facing those charges. The Yard gave him a reference enabling him to gain membership of the Institute of Professional Investigators. He now runs a private investigation agency in Dundee. The medically retired Miller was photographed in his dinner jacket at an IPI function at Gleneagles in 1986 looking in the rudest health.

12 · OPERATION MINDER

WHEN THE 1980s dawned, Roy Garner was as quick as every other gunman in town to see that the golden age of armed robbery had passed. New types of crime beckoned and the professionals moved effortlessly into massive tax frauds and drug dealing. The temptations were overwhelming. Tax fraud carried small penalties for larger rewards than robbery could ever yield. There were big sentences for drug trafficking but the use of couriers made for relatively small risks.

Experience with guns helped, but now they were used to protect the millions in cash and drugs being moved around the streets of London. The only real danger, and the complacent Roy Garner never gave it enough thought, was that tax and drug crimes of the kind he was contemplating were not policed by the Yard but by the civil servants in Her Majesty's Customs and Excise Investigation Department. Garner had no control over them.

From 1980 Garner was dealing in kilos of cocaine under the cover of a North London retail business but, greedy as ever, he resented paying the high margins demanded by the smugglers. He resolved to apply his businessman's brain and become an importer. Being Roy Garner, his venture would have to be the biggest *ever* importation of cocaine.

His business plan was ingenious and merged the most lucrative aspects of both tax frauds and drug importing. First he would need a massive amount of capital, probably several million pounds, in order to trade with the big Colombian dealers. Then he needed a new identity and the false papers that went with it, in order to move this money. Finally he would have to secure a base in Florida, the crossroads of the world's drug routes.

Garner's partner of 20 years, the weasel-like Kenny Ross, was happy to take part in the tax fraud, but after that, he wanted out. The relationship between Garner and Lundy had already been queried in the *Observer* newspaper alongside a photograph of them found in Gibson's house. Garner and Ross had been named in the House of Commons and any more publicity might activate police pressure.

Meanwhile, Garner applied for a new passport in the name of Douglas Henry Stilwell, a milkman. His son Mark, then aged nineteen, was ready to follow in his father's footsteps. He applied for a passport in the name of Tony Barrows, meat porter. An elderly West London doctor was persuaded to authenticate Roy and Mark Garner's applications and a crooked solicitor, Harold Margolis, also helped out.

Garner and the other criminals who stole the Value Added Tax on gold have much to thank Mrs Thatcher for. One of the first acts of her new government in 1979 had been to remove the VAT from gold coins so ordinary people could trade in the precious metal. The ordinary criminals saw the loophole within months, dived through it and stole approaching £1 billion from the Treasury.

Garner's variation on the scam worked like this. Anyone importing less than £50,000 worth of gold coins at one time — the favourites were Krugerrands — was exempted from paying the 15 per cent VAT at Customs. When the coins were sold, the bullion houses of the City gave them the value of the gold plus the 15 per cent tax.

Under the delayed accounting rules, that tax should have been repaid to HM Customs within three months. The capital's hardened robbers gave up their guns overnight and became gold importers, brought in the gold tax-free in the name of bogus front companies and then disappeared with the 15 per cent VAT. The pioneer was Mickey Green, who cleared £6 million and departed happily for Spain. His name would be linked later with Garner's cocaine conspiracy and Nikolaus Chrastny.

Garner joined the Great Gold Swindle in August 1982. In just two months of almost daily return flights to Jersey he and his team, carrying £49,000 worth of Krugerrands each, imported more than £14 million worth of the coins. In the end they had ripped off £2 million that should have been paid in tax. But from the start Garner and Ross had been spotted by Customs and Excise men. They set up 'Operation Minder' and took 2,000 photographs of the swindle in action.

The Customs investigators conferred with both the Stagg and Albany teams at the Met and were given some remarkable advice by the detectives. 'Good luck, don't tell us what you are doing and when you are going to make arrests — in case there's a leak at the Yard. And one other thing; whatever you do, use static observations not mobiles. If Garner spots your cars he can get the numbers checked quickly by his friends at the Yard.'

Roy and Mark Garner, Kenny Ross and two couriers were arrested at Gatwick airport, deliberately outside the Metropolitan Police area, just before Easter 1983. It was nothing more than a textbook investigation. The Customs Officers' success at their first attempt to nail Garner only underlined that he was not a particularly clever criminal, merely a protected one.

Four days after the arrests Jeff Edwards revealed in the *News of the World*:

> Detectives investigating a corruption scandal involving the reward from Britain's biggest ever silver robbery believe they are on the verge of a major breakthrough.
>
> For 18 months the hand-picked Scotland Yard squad have been probing claims that £310,000 fell into the hands of a crooked syndicate. Last week five men and a woman were arrested in a North London raid by other officers investigating a £1.5 million smuggling racket. Now the Yard's internal anti-corruption squad are convinced that they are on the threshold of getting vital information to help crack the bullion case.
>
> They believe they will soon bring charges in what could be the Metropolitan Police's biggest ever corruption scandal —with repercussions at the highest level.

Edwards had clearly been fed by detectives who were keen to see both Stagg and Albany brought to a head. But Garner sat tight in custody and wouldn't talk to Gerry Wiltshire, who spent three days interviewing him. Garner, as ever, had solicitor Pelly at his side.

After two weeks he and Ross were bailed on sureties of £375,000 and Mark Garner on £270,000. Total bail for all six defendants made a Guinness Book of Records total of £1,180,000. A hefty chunk of the money was put up by Sean McCormack, owner of the fashionable Ship Inn on the towpath at Hammersmith. It would be the usual long wait before they appeared at the Old Bailey. In the meantime Garner was about to be forced on to the front pages of the national press. It was an unpleasant experience.

To its own surprise, Operation Albany at last got Garner into court. Harry Clement's team had been amazed to discover that, despite Garner's appalling record as a gunman in the Yard's Criminal Intelligence files, he and his brother David both held shotgun licences. Roy and his son Mark also had licences for .22 rifles. They claimed the shotguns were for shooting over their land at Wormley and the rifles were used for target practice at gun clubs.

What outraged Clement was that Garner wanted even more guns: two more rifles, three automatic pistols and, worst of all, two .357 Magnum pistols, the most formidable handgun in the world. His brother David made a similar request. At Clement's initiative the Yard revoked their licences. Incensed at this intrusion into their right to bear arms, the brothers lodged an appeal. The Garners seemed not to have anticipated what they were letting themselves in for: in a normal court case only tangible evidence can be introduced, in a licence appeal there are no such constraints.

When the case opened in May 1983 Roy Garner withdrew because he had just been charged with the VAT fraud, but he made himself available to support his brother David who persisted with the appeal. It was a fatal mistake. Within minutes of the case beginning David was all but forgotten and the hearing became Roy versus the Met.

The first witness was DAC David Powis, who summarised Operation Albany's findings on Roy Garner. 'I consider him to be a close associate of organised habitual criminals that are preying on the public.' An intense inquiry was going on into allegations against Garner of 'crimes of violence, mainly robberies, arsons and conspiracy to pervert the course of justice in a murder inquiry and similar serious matters. It could never be in the public interest for either Roy or David Garner to possess any firearm. It would be a danger to public safety and the peace.'

With that Powis returned to his fifth-floor office at the Yard leaving mayhem behind him. Although he mentioned having had contact with Garner, he did not reveal the circumstances — the payment of large rewards to the criminal. Neither did he reveal that Albany had been aborted once.

Powis's outburst made the front page of the national press. The *Sun* set the pace. The whole of its front page was devoted to the headline 'Branded' and a picture of Roy and David Garner. Every other paper followed with detailed quotes on Garner's alleged gangsterism. Within days even *The Times* could put Garner's name in a headline and expect readers to know who he was. To avoid the press photographers each morning Garner resorted to climbing over a wall and sprinting for the sanctuary of the court. For the remaining four days of evidence the press bench was packed.

Next to give evidence was Gerry Wiltshire, who said that Garner associated with 'the top criminals in London today' and that the Garner name 'wields quite a surprising amount of power'.

It was Day Three before Garner went into the witness box on brother David's behalf. He was questioned about the finances of Wormley and Elton's and the cost of Cannon Lodge. Few of the figures he gave made sense. He insisted he had built his empire on bank loans and his skills as an astute businessman.

Under pressure he stuck to this nonsense and declared: 'No large sum has been introduced to me in my life.' He claimed his total income was about £25,000 a year. How then, enquired counsel, could he afford to pay £1,100 a month mortgage on his house. 'I've been with NatWest for 26 years' was the best Garner could manage. The judge was not convinced and the Garner gun appeal failed.

Outside the court an angry Garner spat at waiting journalists. 'If I am a murderer, robber and arsonist, what am I doing free?'

In the witness box Garner had let slip some interesting information about another aspect of his complex relationships with the Met. He said that he had given a police officer, Detective Sergeant Peter Docherty, who was a fellow member of Garner's Masonic Lodge, permission to walk on the land at Wormley and shoot. 'I walked round with him and I became interested in shooting. He bought a couple of guns along. He obtained a shotgun which I bought and he assisted me in applying for the certificate. I purchased a number of guns through him.'

Docherty was, of course, the officer who had been told by Harry Clement to sever his connections with Garner, who had been 'truculent' and had disobeyed the order. Docherty later showed all the solidarity to be expected from a fellow Freemason. He admitted that he kept a small caravan at Wormley and added, 'Everybody knows, I would say even the fucking Commissioner knows, that I shoot on his land.' Docherty also claimed there was no truth in rumours of Garner's criminality, despite the damning records held by the Yard.

'What happened was, when I was at C1, I thought [why] all this interest in this fellow so I went up to Criminal Intelligence and had a look at the thing, I said, this is wrong . . . ' Commenting on Powis's allegations that Garner was a major criminal, Docherty continued, 'Do you want my honest opinion, I don't think he is, I really don't think he is, that's my own personal opinion.

'Another thing that annoys me, there's somebody being put down and put down and not being given the opportunity to defend himself. Everybody is making out that Roy Garner is a villain and I've spoken to lots and lots of policemen who know him far, far better than I do and they say, take no notice.' His role as Garner's gun supplier did not damage Docherty's career.

Garner's £2 million gold trial opened at the Old Bailey in November 1984. He was the only defendant, Ross and the others pleaded guilty. All were represented by solicitor Roland Pelly. Garner was desperate not to go to prison. More than at any other time in his life he needed to be at liberty. Six months earlier he had taken the first step in the deal to ship the biggest ever quantity of cocaine into Britain. It would be much more difficult to continue the planning from jail.

To draw fire away from Garner, one of his gang who was pleading guilty went into the witness box and provocatively claimed that he had made off with £1 million of the stolen VAT and was not going to reveal where it was. Judge Richard Lowry was so annoyed by this tactic that he immediately revoked Garner's bail. The trial was endangered by two attempts to nobble the jury but the prosecution pressed on and Garner was convicted.

Passing sentence, Judge Lowry mourned the inadequate penalties for such huge swindles. Then he jailed Garner for two consecutive, two-year maximum periods in prison, fined him £150,000, imposed costs of £90,000 and topped it all up with a Criminal Bankruptcy order to the sum of £1.9 million. Mark Garner received a shorter jail term and was also made bankrupt.

Garner was aghast at the maximum sentence. On the eve of his trial he had met in secret with Lundy and another senior officer to ask for help. The Met followed the usual procedure for secret informants and sent a letter to Lowry asking for leniency. The judge was unimpressed.

Six months later the Appeal Court reduced Garner's four-year sentence to three years. It also quashed his fine. The Appeal Court judges said that the Criminal Bankruptcy orders should be suitable punishment and expressed the hope that 'the full armoury contained in the insolvency legislation will be deployed rigorously against these defendants with as much expedition as possible'.

While Garner was in prison Gerry Wiltshire, now promoted to Superintendent, and in charge of Operation Albany, heard about the false passports. He charged Roy Garner, who pleaded guilty at Wood Green Crown Court in 1986. Again the Yard hierarchy secretly submitted a letter to the judge pleading for leniency. This time it worked and Garner's nine-month sentence ran concurrently with his fraud sentence. He did not have to serve one extra day in jail.

The Yard did its best to ease the pain of Garner's jail sentence. Behind the scenes it put pressure on the Home Office to ensure that he spent most of his time in modern prisons. And unlike other convicts, Garner did not spend all of his sentence behind bars. Within a short while of Garner going away *Daily Express* reporter Tony Dawe revealed: 'Jailed Garner Out On Jaunt.' His story said that Garner had 'just enjoyed a weekend jaunt only months after being jailed for 3 years. He went to look over his racehorses and see his girlfriend at the Hertfordshire estate.'

Under pressure, the Home Office said Garner would have been entitled to two periods of home leave nearer the end of his sentence. This privilege was 'brought forward because of domestic circumstances'. The truth was that Garner urgently needed to be out of prison to supervise the disposal of the £500,000 Wormley estate and his string of racehorses before the Official Receiver closed in.

An MP queried the amazing charity extended to Garner and the minister who replied was Lord Glenarthur. His letter was mindboggling. 'Mr Garner is unwilling to have any information about his treatment whilst serving this sentence divulged to you and I feel bound to respect his wishes.'

In his article Dawe also got to grips with the rigour of Garner's criminal bankruptcy order. Under the headline 'Scandal Of Crooks' Great Loot Loophole' he wrote:

> The futility of criminal bankruptcy was demonstrated vividly a few days ago in an interview room at Ford open prison. Face to face were Roy Garner, 48, once labelled 'a major figure in serious crime in Britain' and jailed last year for a £2 million VAT fraud and Official Receiver Chris Nutting. Nutting's target: an outstanding £1.3 million.
>
> But when Nutting questioned Garner — and his solicitor Roland Pelly — he was told; the family home was mortgaged up to the hilt; the stud farm belonged to Garner's father, a retired market porter; Garner's share of the sale of Elton's went to repay a huge debt on the club and the reward money has been spent.

13 · MEET MR FLYNN

ROY GARNER HAD MOVED more than £1 million of the profits from the gold fraud out of the country before he went down the steps at the Old Bailey to start his jail sentence. Throughout 1983 and early 1984, while on bail and waiting for the case to be heard, he had travelled to Florida, opening new bank accounts and looking for a secure base from which to launch the next stage of his plans.

In the spring of 1984, Garner and his son Mark went back to Florida again. With his stake money well out of reach of the British authorities he was ready to start doing business — big drugs business. This time Garner took his girlfriend. Corinne Clark had shared Garner's bed after starting work as a 16-year-old groom at his Holborn Stud Farm. Soon she became his full-time mistress and together they travelled the world.

Garner's behaviour on these foreign jaunts often surprised the teenager. He always booked the flight tickets in false names. Sometimes he called himself Douglas Stilwell, sometimes Roy Warren and other times he was Ronald Fisher. When they reached a foreign airport he insisted that they queued separately for customs and immigration checks. At the airport car hire desk he would ask Corinne to use her driving licence and pay with one of the credit cards he had obtained for her, giving her the cash when the time came to settle the accounts. According to Corinne,

'I never understood the reasons for this but as it was no hardship, I did as he asked.'

In Florida, Garner and his girlfriend had nothing but the best. On their early trips they stayed in Miami's top hotels, the Hilton, the Sheraton and the Fontainbleu. Then, in the spring of 1984, they moved into a luxurious waterfront apartment at Pompano Beach, fifty miles north of Miami. Garner paid $250,000 for the property. It had three bedrooms, three bathrooms and a vast entertaining area with a huge mirrored wall on one side. Up on the seventh floor the sliding picture windows opened out on to a balcony with a fine view over the Atlantic. Garner and Corinne visited one of Florida's leading interior décor businesses, handed over $30,000, and told them to furnish it.

Hundreds of square feet of cream shag pile carpet were laid throughout the apartment. On top of this stood huge sofas, glass-topped coffee and dining tables and crane-like chromium standard lamps. The co-ordinated colour scheme was in pink and cream.

Pompano Beach and the adjoining city of Fort Lauderdale are typical Florida resorts, with mile upon mile of hotels, exclusive beach-front apartments, marinas with their small navies of exotic pleasure craft and hundreds of bustling bars and restaurants. It was in one such Fort Lauderdale bar, where Oakland Boulevard meets Atlantic, that Roy Garner bumped into Roy Whitehorne.

Whitehorne was one of a growing number of British criminals who had migrated to enjoy the climate and the criminal opportunities on offer in Florida. He had grown up in Sheffield but left the dying steel city to travel the world, first in the Navy and then as a jewel smuggler. He and Roy Garner had a common friend in England in the 1960s. The two men got together several times that spring.

Whitehorne sometimes took his girlfriend Peggee Burrows to Garner's waterfront apartment for lazy poolside barbecues. According to Peggee, 'It was the biggest and most beautiful condominium that I have ever seen.'

Peggee had trained as a beautician and soon made friends with Corinne. She offered to do a make-up demonstration for her in the apartment one afternoon. It was a great success and Corinne ordered several hundred dollars' worth of cosmetics.

When Garner found out he slashed the order back to a mere $40. Peggee thought that was 'pretty mean'.

Roy Whitehorne was a regular caller at the condominium. The apartment block has an elaborate security system and visitors must report to a uniformed guard stationed by a bank of video screens inside the entrance lobby. Before the guard lets them enter the lift they have to be approved by the resident. According to Whitehorne, 'On all the occasions that I had called I was always directed to go straight up to the apartment. On one occasion, however, I was asked to stay downstairs in the lobby. I was later apologized to for being kept waiting and told that there were some people in the apartment I did not need to see. I was later told that the people were "Old Bill". It wasn't important for me to know who the "Old Bill" were so I didn't pursue it.'

Garner soon discovered that Whitehorne was a regular visitor to Colombia. He began to prompt the garrulous Yorkshireman about his activities there and who his contacts were. Eventually, as Garner had hoped, Whitehorne revealed that he had a contact in Florida who was looking for partners in Europe to invest in large-scale cocaine smuggling. Garner told him that he was well-connected with people in London who were keen to buy the drug and pressed Whitehorne to arrange a meeting with his Florida contact. When Garner was told that the contact would only deal on a cash basis, Whitehorne remembers him replying that he could produce '"one, two, three million pounds in cash if required". I said that on that basis I would arrange a meeting.'

Apart from his German accent Charles Albert Flynn seemed to be a typical middle-aged American businessman. Flynn claimed to have been born in Orlando, Florida, in 1944, and now, with his wife and small son, was living in a sprawling bungalow with a pool at the back and a Mercedes parked at the front. At around 5'9" tall, balding, bearded and bespectacled, there was nothing about his appearance to indicate that Flynn was one of the most wanted men in the world.

The house off Griffin Road, in Broward County, had been chosen for its isolation. Set well back from a dusty unmade road, it was bordered by thickset trees and bushes. It was almost impossible for any inquisitive law enforcement agency to put the house under close surveillance. Neighbours who noticed the

100-foot-tall radio mast in the grounds assumed that Flynn was a radio ham.

The beard, the glasses and the hairstyle could be changed at will; Flynn constantly need to adjust his identity. The real Charles Albert Flynn had died in 1946 at the age of two. The man who had so successfully assumed the dead child's name was Nikolaus Maria Chrastny. He had been born illegitimately in Troppeau, Czechoslovakia, in 1943 and was on the run from his adopted country, the Federal Republic of Germany.

Chrastny grew up on an isolated farm in Bavaria. He claims that when he was young he was expelled from a college run by Catholic priests. His crime was to cast doubts on the Bible. According to Chrastny, 'I asked how Noah was able, in the Palestine desert, to take a penguin on board the Ark.'

By the age of eighteen he was regularly dabbling in small scale burglary and theft. The law caught up with him after he mugged a taxi driver one night because 'I was in love with a nurse and needed money for a hotel room'. His night of passion cost him an 18-month prison sentence in Landsberg am Lech.

There was something about women in uniform that clearly appealed to the young criminal and in 1970 he married Charlotte Schreiber, then a policewoman in Munich. She did not prove to be a good influence and three years later the local detectives were hunting him after a jewel robbery in the city. According to the police, Chrastny walked into a jeweller's shop in Munich and told the owner, 'I want to convert some funds into diamonds.' When the jeweller produced the gems, Chrastny took out a revolver and departed with £250,000 worth of stones. Chrastny's own version is rather different. 'I didn't need a pistol at the time,' he claimed, 'the jeweller and I were friends. I got to know the man in a wine bar in Rheinland-Pfalz. We shared the proceeds and I was given a headstart before he raised the alarm.'

Chrastny fled all the way across the Atlantic. 'I went to the USA and pawned the jewellery for $60,000,' he claimed. 'In Florida I got to know a former US soldier who took me to Jamaica.' That was his introduction to the drug trade, and according to Chrastny he earned $10,000 on his first smuggling trip. He also earned the respect of the big-league smugglers and was soon trusted to ride shotgun on loads of Colombian marijuana being delivered all over the country. Within a couple of years Chrastny had learned all he needed to know. 'In 1975

I pinched a charter boat in Grenada and set up business on my own.' On the way to becoming his own boss Chrastny changed his identity and became Charles Albert Flynn.

Chrastny made big profits and spent them wisely. He started dealing in precious stones and became a regular visitor at a jewellery store called Lords of London in Tamarac, Florida. The proprietor was Roy Whitehorne. They became friends and later Whitehorne was to boast that 'Charles and I sailed round half the world together'.

They resolved to find their own sources of precious stones and set up expeditions to Colombia. Whitehorne always insisted that their journeys into the mountains were nothing to do with drug smuggling. He tells elaborate stories of them recruiting their own private army of twenty gunmen, travelling up-country to the dangerous emerald mines, bargaining for the precious stones and then fighting their way back home with the contraband.

Peggee Burrows, Whitehorne's girlfriend, was less sure about Flynn. She always found him to be a perfect gentleman but was unnerved by tales of his exploits. Whitehorne told her that Flynn was a crack shot, the best sailor he had ever met and had been involved in at least one murder.

Everyone who did business with Flynn had two distinct impressions of him. On the one hand he always kept his word, paid what he owed and never put them in jeopardy with the law. But they were all in awe of him. Flynn would make a point at some stage in every relationship of behaving in a terrifyingly violent way. At a moment of his own choosing he would explode with rage, smashing furniture and firing bullets into the walls behind them. He was not a man to cross.

The only man never to learn that lesson was Roy Garner. All he could see before him in the spring of 1984 was a man who shared his current obsession. They both wanted to put together Europe's biggest ever drug deal.

East Commercial Boulevard is a six-lane highway that runs from the Atlantic shoreline inland through the miles of neon-lit shopping malls and suburban residential areas that are typical of Florida's Broward County. Number 2744 is a single-storey corner block on the coastal end of the boulevard and by the spring of 1984 Roy Whitehorne had moved there to open a new business, named Brasilliance. When he finally told Roy Garner that he could meet his cocaine smuggling contact, the jewellery store seemed the most discreet setting.

Garner and his son Mark arrived at Brasilliance first. They waited for a while and, when Flynn failed to show up, they went off for a meal in one of the many restaurants on the north side of the boulevard.

Charles Flynn was waiting when they returned. Whitehorne made the introductions. According to Flynn, 'I shook hands with each of those gentlemen. Roy Garner's handshake struck me like shaking hands with an eel.' Flynn explained that he wanted to expand his cocaine operation and was looking to Europe. He felt that the European coastguards and law enforcement agencies were far less professional than their American counterparts and he could successfully do business. He also knew he could make a much bigger profit; European street prices for cocaine were much higher than in the US.

The discussion of prices and amounts lasted only twenty minutes. Garner assured Flynn that his group was well connected in London and that he would have no difficulties in moving large quantities of cocaine. Flynn was less sure. The secret of his success, and the fact that after a decade of smuggling drugs throughout America he was still unknown to the authorities, was all down to precise planning. He left little to chance.

Flynn believed in getting hold of as much inside information as possible. He always wanted to know what the other side was up to. Now that he was breaking into a new market he was particularly keen to find out as much as he could. He was frank with Garner about his concerns. The answer he got was a drug smuggler's dream.

Flynn recalled telling Garner that 'From a professional point of view I had my doubts moving into an area where the infrastructure, by that I mean the intelligence to do a job professionally, was a complete unknown to me. He told me that his group was getting information about necessary intelligence directly from the Yard. He also told me that whatever will be going on, we will know exactly about it.

'I asked in detail, how he was going to manage to give me inside information as far as was necessary to do the job. I cannot overstress the importance of those talks at this time because it is vital for any enterprise of this kind to know as much about your opposition as possible.

'After talking with me for a while and because I was not interested in vague statements and because I impressed on him that I had to be conscientious of the security of all the people involved, he gave me the name of Mr Lundy. I checked this name out with my FBI contacts. The message came back to me that there was actually such a man very high up in Scotland Yard.'

14 · ELEPHANTS AND COCAINE

CHRASTNY HAD HIS doubts about Roy Garner from the start. Garner sensed the international drug smuggler's unease and kept assuring him that he would have no difficulties moving large quantities of cocaine. Three years later, in a secret confession to British Customs officers, Chrastny reflected on that first meeting with Garner. 'I should have been more sceptical,' he admitted.

But the lure of breaking into the big-time in Britain was too much. Chrastny decided that he would do business with Garner, and when Whitehorne heard later in April 1984 that his British partner wanted to meet 'Mr Flynn' again, but this time on his home turf, Chrastny agreed to fly to London.

The conspirators' first meeting was to be held at the discreet Athenaeum Hotel in Piccadilly. Garner sent an associate who explained that his boss wanted to stay in the background. First he told Chrastny about the mechanics of their cocaine distribution operations. Garner had developed an ingenious system using London taxicabs, fitted with secret compartments to hold the cocaine. Then he put Chrastny's mind at rest again about the safety of the operations. He repeated the assurances first made by Garner in Florida. Should any problems develop, they would be alerted by their police contact.

Two further planning meetings were held in London that year. The venue moved from the up-market Athenaeum Hotel to the very down-market Circle Club in Palmers Green. The Circle was an after-hours drinking club owned by Garner and his brother David. It was the haunt of London criminals and came under police surveillance frequently throughout the 1980s.

Garner was in the chair at the Circle Club meetings. According to Whitehorne, he was still at great pains to assure Chrastny that 'their police contacts could take care of most things'. Three of these contacts were mentioned, two by their first names, which Whitehorne could not recall. But he was certain about the third name. 'The one I definitely remember was Tony Lundy.'

Now it was time for the conspirators to get down to details. Garner would have to pay $35,000 for every kilo of cocaine delivered to him in London. According to Chrastny, 'we more or less decided that I would deliver an unspecified but large amount to his group'. All that remained was for Garner to give a sign of good faith. Chrastny told him the number of an account at a bank in Panama and asked for a deposit of approximately $100,000, to be paid as soon as possible. Within days Garner credited the Panamanian account with $70,000. This was then forwarded to the Colombian cocaine suppliers in Medellín. Garner foolishly noted the payment on a piece of paper that he left in one of his North London homes; '£53,000 to Fritz.'

Back in Florida, Chrastny still had doubts about his new British partner. He decided to set him a test. Whitehorne was given a message to pass to Garner. He must get together a further £1 million in cash. This was more of an irritation than a problem for a man of Garner's wealth. The bundles of cash were hidden at Cannon Lodge and Garner waited for further instructions, but the scheduled contact time came and went with no message from America. Finally Whitehorne received an irate call from London. Taking £1 million out of the system on Chrastny's say-so was no simple matter, he was told. Garner, apparently, was furious. When Whitehorne passed on the message, Chrastny simply laughed. He held all the cards.

Garner had warned Chrastny that later in 1984 he might go to jail over the gold swindle. Chrastny's passport, in the name of Flynn, shows that he visited London during the trial and Customs officers believe that he actually sat in the public gallery of Court 12 at the Old Bailey one day during the hearing. It was to the credit of his new partner that he could steal as much as £1.9 million. Chrastny was impressed — he decided to continue his plans for the cocaine venture. The next stage was to obtain the best boat for the smuggling voyage.

Early in 1985 an advertisement in a yachting magazine caught his eye. It was for a boat called the *Aquilon*, then berthed in Rhodes. She was described as 'a former North Sea pilot vessel. With her economy, accommodation, range and sea-worthiness she could cruise the world'. As important to Chrastny, as Customs officers were told later, was the fact that 'you could hide elephants in her'. In Chrastny's stilted English, 'It seemed at least on paper that she had the properties to do the desired job.' He flew to Greece, examined the boat and agreed a price of £55,000.

The *Aquilon* was sailed to the port of Piraeus for a full survey. Once satisfied by the report, Chrastny paid the balance of the price and registered her to a company he had set up in the Channel Islands. A crew was hired for the long trip westwards. They sailed first to Gibraltar, then on to Grand Canary and Barbados. Here they were joined by a young man called Martin Schreiber. One of his shipmates described him as 'your basic punk, tattooed, tall, skinny, real short hair'. Schreiber soon proved to have thoroughly unpleasant interests. One was a fascination for Nazi memorabilia; another was for guns. He brought two rifles aboard when he joined the *Aquilon* in the West Indies, and later, in Britain, he searched the army surplus stores until he found a World War Two German flame thrower. Martin Schreiber, it turned out, was Chrastny's brother-in-law.

The *Aquilon* sailed out of the West Indies and on to Central America. She went through the Panama Canal and northwards up the coast of Costa Rica to Puntarenas. There she berthed in a private boat yard owned by Eggert Kronby, Chrastny's trusted Danish skipper. Here they began work refitting the *Aquilon* with larger fuel tanks for her voyage to Britain. The new tanks would hold a lot more than diesel fuel; within them were the secret compartments for the cocaine.

Chrastny based himself at the Amstel Hotel in the Costa Rican capital of San José and divided his time between checking on the progress of the work at the Puntarenas boat yard and travelling to Colombia to negotiate for the drugs. It was Chrastny's boast that he went to the top; his dealings were with the notorious

Ochoa family, leaders of the Medellín cocaine cartel. Not only was he on first name terms with the Ochoas, he was also an associate of another Medellín cocaine baron, Pablo Escobar.

The consignment for Britain was negotiated with 'Uncle Alberto' of the Ochoa clan who clearly approved of Chrastny's plan to export to Britain. According to Chrastny, 'I originally planned on getting between 150 and 200 kilos of cocaine, but they liked the idea of opening a further European market so much that they asked me how much I could take. I ended up with 392 kilos.' Chrastny paid the Ochoas $190,000 for the first 38 kilos. The rest of the drugs were 'fronted' on credit. The Ochoas knew two key things about Chrastny: he had been trustworthy in the past, and it needed a man of his special talents to open up the new market. That they would let him sail away into the Atlantic with 354 kilos of their best quality cocaine on credit showed just how highly they rated him.

Chrastny had done his homework on the British weather and tides. He decided that there was only one time of year when he could risk a successful landing in Britain. He called it a 'window of weather' and he reckoned it was the three-month period from July to September. That 'window' would open in the summer of 1986.

On American Independence Day, 4 July 1986, the *Aquilon* slipped out of the Christobal Yacht Club in Panama on the start of her voyage to England. Secreted in her fuel tanks was £100 million worth of Colombian cocaine. It had taken the crew four days to wrap and conceal the illegal cargo in the *Aquilon*'s hidden compartments.

Behind them they left Paul Caruso, a young American drifter who had been hired by Chrastny to baby-sit another of his boats. He recalled being approached a week later by a Colombian who introduced himself simply as 'George'. 'He asked me if I had seen Charles Flynn. He said he was supposed to contact him some two weeks earlier as he had over $1 million of his goods which were worth $8 million in Miami. I realised then that these guys were into big-time drugs of some kind. I said that I had not seen him since he left for London on 4 July. He was very unhappy and annoyed. He then left.'

A week after the anxious inquiry from the sinister Colombian, Flynn was to be found in room 1078 at the London Tara

Hotel. Registered with him were two other American guests, Lee Bryan and Brian Van der Breen. Bryan was Chrastny's longtime partner; his real name was Leopold Strohschein and he too was a German exile. Van der Breen was a self-confessed yacht bum who hoped to earn enough from the smuggling trip to Britain to buy a catamaran to take him round the world.

Two days later, the three men hired a blue Fiat Regatta and set off to tour the South of England. They went right down to Land's End, stopping at different points along the coast. Tourism was the last thing on their minds: they were checking out likely landing sites for the cocaine.

On their return to London the three men rented a flat in Roebuck House, part of a huge concrete complex in Victoria, just around the corner from Scotland Yard. The flat at Roebuck House was to become the first London safe house for the biggest importation of cocaine Britain has ever seen.

Early in August Van der Breen was given responsibility for the next stage of the plan. He bought a selection of yachting magazines and started making phone calls. Finally he came up with a catamaran, the *Katlyn*, that was available for immediate hire.

With a contract for a month's charter in his pocket Van der Breen sailed *Katlyn* to Falmouth and met up with Martin Schreiber. They installed additional radio equipment and made contact with the *Aquilon*, now only a few days away from British waters.

Chrastny briefed the two men endlessly, taking them over his plans to meet the *Aquilon* at sea and tranship the cocaine to the *Katlyn*. The appointed rendezvous was 30 miles due south of Falmouth. Schreiber was now speaking to the approaching *Aquilon* twice-daily on the new radio equipment, while Van der Breen took the catamaran out on regular runs around the Lizard to get familiar with the waters.

In the early hours of 20 August 1986 the *Aquilon* finally passed the Lizard and hove to, feigning engine trouble. The *Katlyn*, which had set out from Falmouth, stopped about 150 yards away. Suddenly Eggert Kronby, the skipper of the *Aquilon*, appeared out of the darkness in a Zodiac rubber dinghy. He had with him two heavy-duty plastic sacks which he hauled across to the *Katlyn*. According to Van der Breen 'I thought we were finished but he said, "There's more."' Once again the rubber dinghy crossed between *Aquilon* and the *Katlyn* ferrying its contraband. Once again the cocaine-stuffed sacks were handed over. Martin Schreiber shoved them under the *Katlyn*'s two bunk beds and Van der Breen steered as they sailed back towards the dawn and the safety of the shore.

At 9.12 that morning a light aircraft climbed into the sky above the Cornwall coast. Strapped safely into the passenger seat was Nikolaus Chrastny. Through his binoculars Chrastny soon spotted the *Katlyn* making her way back to an anchorage buoy he had rented on the Helford River. Chrastny raised the *Katlyn* on the radio, assured her that he had heard nothing of concern on the frequencies he had been monitoring and that from his airborne position there were 'no hostile forces in sight'.

Around midday Martin Schreiber launched a small rubber boat from the *Katlyn*, by now moored at the anchorage buoy, and motored ashore. Waiting on the quay was Chrastny, who handed him twenty duffle bags. Over the next three days Schreiber and Van der Breen were kept busy filling a couple of the bags at a time with drugs, boarding the rubber dinghy and casually ferrying the cocaine ashore. Once on dry land the two men handed over the bags to Chrastny. They moved steadily around the jetties of the estuary, never using the same handover point twice. With the cocaine packed tightly into the boots of three hired cars, they set off in convoy on the long drive up to London. Late in the day they arrived at the rented flat in Victoria and put the cocaine gently to rest.

The whole operation, once the cocaine had been picked up from the *Aquilon*, had been carried out in daylight and in full public view. It had all gone remarkably well. Indeed, according to Chrastny, there had only been one little problem, and that was on the drive up to London. 'I think it was a Bank Holiday;' he said, 'the traffic was terrible.'

15 · THE SUNSHINE STATE

TWENTY YEARS POLICING the streets of New York was enough for Mike Minto. He had fought the Mafia families as they built up their heroin networks and worked on state-wide investigations into police corruption. He had seen all sides of a detective's work. After two decades Minto qualified for a pension and, handing his Captain's badge back to the New York State police, headed south for Florida. When asked why he left the energy and buzz of the world's most exciting city he laughs: 'You seen the winters in Brooklyn?'

Minto is deceptively easy-going. Other detectives might run after their quarry; Minto appears to stroll — but he always gets there. He learned his trade tracking and arresting Mafia boss Tommaso Buscetta in New York in 1970, fifteen years before the Palermo Godfather became the Mob's biggest ever supergrass. For Minto the joy of starting a second career with the Florida Department of Law Enforcement was that it put him back on the streets, practising basic detective and intelligence-gathering work.

The FDLE is the detective branch of the State Police. Its Special Agents concentrate on two kinds of crime, fraud and drugs. America's fraudsmen, phoney share dealers and crooked accountants have made new homes in resort cities like Fort Lauderdale and West Palm Beach. When they are not stealing money, they are laundering it. The financial operators are never short of clients because they provide special services to Florida's other major criminal culture: the suppliers, shippers, distributors, dealers and users who together make up the drugs trade with which the name of Florida has now become synonymous.

In his new job Special Agent Mike Minto quietly cruised the bars of the Sunshine State, drinking coffee, making friends and listening. The Medellín Mafia had a new and capable enemy. Strapped to his ankle was a snub-nosed revolver, worn, but never fired, for 28 years. After five years in the sunshine of South Florida, Minto found himself based at the FDLE's discreet single-storey offices in Pompano Beach. He was working with a new and younger partner, Mike Breece. In December 1984 they listened patiently to a frightened woman who wanted to give them information in secret.

She had walked out on her boyfriend, she said, after discovering that he was mixing with major criminals. She suspected that some of them were drug traffickers. The woman's name was Peggee Burrows and her boyfriend was the British expatriate jeweller Roy Whitehorne.

Minto and Breece began watching Whitehorne, his associates and his jewellery store on East Commercial Boulevard. Early on they managed, surreptitiously, to snatch a photograph of a bespectacled man driving away in his Mercedes. The problem was to identify him and the other dubious characters who wandered in and out of Brasilliance.

Their surveillance would eventually trigger a string of similar investigations around the world. They code-named their efforts 'Operation Internos' and watched their inquiries grow until Minto realised that they had spread 'to every state of the Union'. In time the investigation would vault the Atlantic, taking with it allegations of corruption which reached to the very heart of Scotland Yard.

Jimmy Tullevere provided the answer to Minto and Breece's surveillance problem. He was in jail, he did not like it and he wanted to trade his way out. Tullevere was a skilled and persistent thief. He specialised in trawling the upmarket hotels of Florida's East Coast looking for likely victims. His ideal targets were those elderly, single women who looked as if they might have worthwhile jewellery collections. Once selected, he would stake out his target, wait for her to leave the hotel, break into the room and take what he could find.

Tullevere made a stark offer to Special Agent Mike Breece. If he could be allowed out of jail he would infiltrate the gang of Breece's choice. If he got results then, hopefully, his jail sentence might be shortened. Eighteen months later Tullevere had performed so well and vacuumed up so much high-grade criminal intelligence that he was accepted on to the Federal Witness Protection Programme and, far from being in jail, was living under police protection.

His special talent was his acting ability. Minto described their infiltrator as a 'bit of a ham'. His plausible manner had served Tullevere well when he patrolled the hotel corridors looking for victims and now it was to fool Whitehorne and his circle. In the middle of 1985 Tullevere wandered into the Brasilliance jewellery store and struck up a conversation with the owner. Once Whitehorne started talking, it was almost impossible to get him to stop. He talked about his friends and he talked about their criminal plans. Every conversation was being picked up by a small radio microphone worn by Tullevere, sometimes on his ankle, sometimes in his crotch. The radio signals went straight to a receiver operated by FDLE agents listening in a vehicle parked across the street from Whitehorne's shop.

When Whitehorne pleaded guilty in November 1986 to conspiracy to trafficking in cocaine the Florida court heard that there were 125 hours of taped conversations between the two men.

The name of Charles Flynn and the hints of a huge cocaine plot came up early in the Tullevere tapes, but it wasn't until the spring of 1986 that Minto and Breece realised there was a major British involvement in the criminal plans they had uncovered. One name on the tapes particularly interested Minto and Breece. For legal reasons that name cannot be identified: he will be called 'John Smith'. 'Smith' had a London telephone number. Breece and Minto telexed the Interpol Office at Scotland Yard for help. They got no reply. Despite numerous messages the FDLE never received a response.

Fortunately, another FDLE agent, Bruce Nill, had built up a personal relationship with a detective at C6, the Fraud Squad at Scotland Yard. On 24 June 1986 Agent Nill spoke to his contact, explained the problem and asked if he could get things moving. When his contact checked the telephone number, one other piece of information caught his attention. Criminal Intelligence files showed that Smith was already known to the Yard and another officer was logged as having a long-standing interest in him.

Detective Sergeant Gordon Bain has the reputation of being a very determined detective. A diminutive but stocky Scot, he was compared by one of his bosses to 'a bull terrier'. It was common knowledge at the Yard that once Bain got his teeth into something he would never willingly let go. To certain senior officers in Scotland Yard this made Bain a very dangerous detective.

Bain had been an early recruit to the Operation Albany team. Like the rest of the squad, Bain had been amazed when the cases against Garner on the arsons and on the conspiracy to pervert the course of justice in the Raymond Hoy murder case were marked 'insufficient evidence' by the Director of Public Prosecutions. By June 1986 Bain was one of only two detectives who remained on what was left of Operation Albany. In charge was Chief Superintendent John Bates. They worked directly to Scotland Yard's head of Specialist Operations, Deputy Assistant Commissioner Brian Worth.

The intention of the Yard by that time was to close down Operation Albany and quietly bury it. An internal report from Chief Superintendent Bates summarising Operation Albany in September 1986 concluded, 'It is suggested that the police enquiry into the activities of Garner and his associates . . . be suspended pending further specific information coming to light.' Many senior officers were only too happy with this suggestion. It looked as if their top informant and their top detective had survived.

Bain was outraged. He knew all the allegations about Garner and Lundy and he had seen at first hand what happened to the hard work of the decent and honest officers who had investigated them. Bain was determined to bring Garner to justice.

Bain immediately realised the explosive potential of the new information, for 'John Smith' was an associate of Roy Garner. If Smith was in the frame on a cocaine conspiracy then Garner had to be in it too. He also realised that if Garner was involved, then the name of Tony Lundy was likely to crop up as well. Bain was going to have to play a very careful game if he wanted to bring Garner to justice and survive himself.

Bain persuaded his Fraud Squad colleague to write a report to his bosses about the Florida inquiry and make sure that Bain's interest was highlighted. Bain would then have official cover for wishing to contact the Florida investigators.

The report worked its way through the Scotland Yard system just as Bain had planned and two days later a copy arrived on his desk. He talked immediately to Agent Nill at the FDLE and was put in touch with Mike Minto. The two men, on either side of the Atlantic, recognised each other as kindred spirits. Minto told Bain about Whitehorne and Charles Flynn and what he knew of the cocaine plans. Bain told Minto all about Garner. Minto confirmed immediately that the name Garner had indeed come up on the Tullevere tapes.

Bain now had to undertake a delicate and unpleasant task. He knew that once new information about Garner was lodged at the Yard it would only be a matter of time before it found its way back to their top informant. The information about the cocaine investigation must be moved outside the Yard. He went to see his old friend Mike Packham at Customs and Excise. Packham had been the case officer in charge of the investigation into Garner's gold swindle.

He introduced Bain to the Romeos, the code-name for one of the Customs teams which target the cocaine smugglers. Bain told Hughie Donagher, leader of the Romeos, of the information from Florida that plans were under way for a huge cocaine shipment to England. When he told the Romeos that around 700 kilos were expected, they simply didn't believe him. Hunting for 10 kilos was a huge operation to the Romeos at that time. But Bain had achieved his objective: the new information on Garner was now in the hands of another investigating agency, one which was untouched by Scotland Yard's problems with Garner and Lundy. It was also the only investigating agency that had managed to jail Roy Garner in his twenty years as an active criminal.

By the end of July 1986 Bain was ready to submit his first report to the Yard bosses about the cocaine conspiracy. He knew that to make the case against Garner he was going to have to get out to Florida and further his budding relationship with Special Agent Minto. Given the Yard's desire to let Albany die quietly, Bain realised that this would not be easy. He took advice from a senior officer on the drugs squad. Bain was advised to banish Garner's name from the report to his bosses.

This he did. Then he added a final paragraph which alone almost guaranteed Bain a seat on the next flight out to Miami. It read, 'I understand that H.M. Customs and Excise are already planning to send an officer.' This brought the immediate backing of Bain's Commander at C1, Ron Dowling, who wrote, 'Customs sending a representative . . . would in my view be detrimental to any future police operations in this country.' On 1 August, just three weeks before the *Aquilon* was to deliver the biggest ever consignment of cocaine into England, Gordon Bain was given authority to travel to Florida.

16 · HOLLYWOOD VAULTS

SERGEANT BAIN'S REPORT on what he had learned in Florida was awaited eagerly at Scotland Yard. A case conference was organised in mid-August 1986. The Drugs Squad, the Serious Crime Squad and, thanks to Bain's foresight, officers from Customs and Excise were all present. Bain summarised the information from Minto and Breece; they believed that anything up to three-quarters of a ton of cocaine was destined for Britain. For all they knew, the drugs could have arrived already.

It was clearly a massive smuggling operation and so the conference could end with only one decision; the case had to be given to the Customs and Excise Investigation Department. Their Romeos team would lead the hunt. Every investigation by the Romeos is given a name beginning with the letter 'R'. As the information on the cocaine conspiracy had come from America, they code-named it 'Operation Redskin'. In secret the Yard also set up its own operation, code-named 'Distant Drum'.

Bain was instructed to liaise with the Yard, Customs and Excise, the Florida Department of Law Enforcement and, later, the BKA, the West German Police. In all drugs investigations, details of the suspects and their plan are logged on the National Drugs Intelligence Unit computer. Now, to the names of Charles Flynn and Roy Whitehorne was added that of Roy Garner.

Keeping watch on Garner was simple; he was in Wayland prison in Norfolk nearing the end of his sentence for the gold swindle. Roy Whitehorne was in his Fort Lauderdale jewellery shop chatting unknowingly into Jimmy Tullevere's microphone. The problem was that Charles Flynn seemed to have disappeared completely. The Colombians had lost track of him and so had his other partners in the cocaine conspiracy.

The investigators meeting at the Yard would have been horrified had they known that even as they moved to set up their operations that morning, the international drug smuggler was living just a quarter of a mile away. He was busy preparing Flat 104 at Roebuck House to receive 392 kilos of cocaine in ten days' time.

John Smith, the associate of Garner's whose name had turned up on the Florida tapes, had his phone calls intercepted by the Customs officers. Smith had no idea of their interest in him. Neither did he know that 6,000 miles away another set of investigators were also beginning to take an interest.

Larry Bird is a detective with the Robbery and Homicide division of the Los Angeles Police Department. On 1 October 1986 he was listening carefully to an unwilling visitor to Room 324 of the Parker Center in downtown Los Angeles. The visitor was a slightly built and rather odd looking Londoner named Peter Davy. For many years Davy had worn an unnatural ginger-tinted hairpiece. It had earned him the obvious nickname of 'Wiggy'.

Davy was a fraudster with a long criminal record who had first arrived in Los Angeles in 1982. He was a wanted man, and when the British authorities caught up with him two years later, Davy was extradited. Back in Britain he spent 10 months in Wandsworth prison for a VAT fraud. On his release he returned to the United States. Entering through Seattle, on a fraudulently obtained visa, Davy moved back down the West Coast to Los Angeles. He renewed contact with his old associates and went into the second-hand car business.

A few days before Davy was released from Wandsworth prison in January 1986 he bumped into John Smith, who was near the end of a two-year sentence. Smith was consoling himself with the thought that when he got out in a month's time he had over $1 million salted away in a New York bank account. He shared this money, he explained to Davy, with an associate of his called Roy Garner.

Davy told Smith that on his release the following week he was going to return to the States. Smith filed this away for his future use. When Davy did return to Los Angeles he moved in with an old friend in Glencoe Way, Hollywood. He had hardly settled in when, on 20 February, he received a telephone call. It was John Smith in London. Could Davy, asked Smith, give him some urgent help?

Two days before Smith's frantic call to Davy in Los Angeles, Detective Sergeant Gordon Bain had attended Tottenham Magistrates Court in North London for the remand of a prisoner accused of possessing a forged passport. The man in the dock had been brought to the court from prison, where he was serving a three-year sentence for a multi-million pound gold swindle. It was Roy Garner.

Earlier that morning Garner's son, Mark, had left the family mansion at Cannon Lodge, jumped into his BMW, and headed for the court. On his way across North London he stopped off to see Corinne Clark, his father's mistress. She frequently held messages and letters for Garner. Bain was waiting outside the court when Mark Garner arrived. When he saw the young criminal bankrupt arriving in a BMW the red mist came down over the detective's eyes. It was time to give young Mark 'a pull'. The results were remarkable.

The contents of Mark's executive-style briefcase proved to be a turning-point in the war against Garner. There were details of attempts by Garner to outwit the Official Receiver who had been appointed to seize his assets. There were documents revealing Garner's successful disposal of several of his London properties. Alongside was Mark Garner's diary with the home phone number for a prison officer and details of payments to him. And in a notebook were three phone numbers for Tony Lundy, including the special ex-directory one at the detective's home. Most intriguing of all was a set of accounts detailing substantial American investments.

These documents revealed that Roy Garner and his son Mark were the owners of the Caliph Corporation, registered in the Dutch Antilles, in the Caribbean. The business had been set up in 1983 to trade in stocks and shares. It was managed by a firm of consultants on Third Avenue, New York. The Corporation account was also held in New York with the prestigious bankers Lehman Bros, Khun Loeb. There was a balance sheet for the criminals' account. In January 1986, it stood at $1,262,687 and 15 cents.

When Smith called Peter Davy in Los Angeles on 20 February the 'urgent help' he wanted was a speedy removal of the million and a quarter dollars from New York before Sergeant Bain could get hold of it.

Peter Davy is a fraudsman by occupation and his heart missed a beat when Smith begged him to take charge of the money. Davy replied that he would be delighted to help and reported the proposition to a business associate. He suggested that they get some legal advice on the best way to transfer the British criminal's money.

There is a Hollywood attorney who can fix anything for a price. He was more than happy to arrange for Garner's money to disappear — as long as Davy could make it worth his while. The attorney's terms were 10 per cent of the one and a quarter million dollars. This was agreed quickly and then he told Davy to come back to his office the next day, but this time using an assumed name.

Davy duly returned, now under the new name. Following the attorney's instructions he explained that he was about to divorce and wanted to hide some money away from his wife. The Attorney then opened an account at a local bank in the false name.

Once these arrangements had been made, Davy called Smith in London to give him his instructions for moving the money. Smith had been busy. He had liquidated all the assets of the Caliph Corporation and closed down the New York account at Lehman Bros. The money had been quickly transferred to another New York bank, and then wired to the new bank account in Los Angeles.

As the money passed by, the attorney helped himself to $128,000, although he got Davy to sign bogus receipts to show he'd taken just $11,000. He also took a further $10,000 which he said he had to pay to the bank manager who had helped set up the account. Davy and his associate joined in and helped themselves to $124,000

The next day the attorney closed that account and converted

the cash into nearly $1 million worth of gold Krugerrands and Canadian Maple Leaf coins. That afternoon the lawyer and his two accomplices manhandled four boxes heavy with gold into the boot of Davy's car and drove off to a private vault company in Hollywood.

Davy and his associate rented four security boxes and made up an access code from one of their credit card numbers, set up the boxes so that they could only be opened with two separate keys, and walked out into the California sunshine. Within ten days of Mark Garner's briefcase falling into the hands of Sergeant Bain at Tottenham Magistrates Court, one and a quarter million dollars of Garner's criminal profits had been successfully removed from the reach of the British authorities. If Garner had known what was to happen at Scotland Yard in the following days, he need never have bothered.

Sergeant Bain and his boss, Superintendent Gerry Wiltshire, knew they would have to move fast if they were going to intercept the funds in America. If they could get to the money quickly, then for the first time since the Director of Public Prosecutions had written 'insufficient evidence' on the arson and murder cases against Garner, Operation Albany would have a real opportunity of dealing him a devastating blow.

The day after Smith called Davy in Los Angeles to beg his help in moving the money, Bain and Wiltshire went to the office of the Director of Public Prosecutions. They produced the American records found in the briefcase and asked what action could be taken to enforce the criminal bankruptcy orders served on Roy Garner at his trial for the gold swindle. They were told that the DPP's office had no power to act, but that Scotland Yard did. Back at the Yard they were told that no action would be taken.

There were other detectives at the Yard who were as concerned as Bain and Wiltshire about Garner's funds in America; but the nature of their concern was very different. They definitely did not want the money seized and they made their views fearfully clear. After leaving the DPP's office a disconsolate Bain and Wiltshire went for an early evening drink in a pub popular with detectives.

Wiltshire was approached by a Detective Superintendent who raised the subject of Wiltshire's upcoming retirement. A month

1 Nikolaus Chrastny and his wife in Harley Street

2 Chrastny, the master of disguise

3 Deputy Assistant Commissioner David 'Crazy Horse' Powis

4 Roy Garner (left) with Eric Morecambe and Kenny Ross

THE Sun

SUN PICTURE SPECIAL

MY ALANA'S NO PIRANHA

See Page 5

15p

TODAY'S TV: PAGE 14

Di is set to cast her vote!

BRANDED

Club boss is crime's Mr Big, says top Yard man

NIGHTCLUB boss Roy Garner was branded yesterday as a Mr Big of crime.

Scotland Yard's top detective slammed 47-year-old Garner as a key gangland figure who had links with underworld chiefs in America.

By PETER BOND

The branded Garner brothers . . . Roy, left, and David outside the court yesterday

Continued on Page Four

£40,000 BINGO! Lucky numbers on Page 23

5 Roy and David Garner make the front page of the *Sun*

6 Tony Lundy (fourth from right in back row), Roy Garner and Kenny Ross (both far right) at a West End hotel in the 1970s

earlier Wiltshire, who had nearly thirty years' service, had been told that, due to a hearing defect, he was to be placed on terminal leave. According to Wiltshire, the officer who cornered him in the bar suggested that he should stop pursuing Garner's money and added, 'You don't need all this Garner hassle. Why don't you just retire quietly to Wales?' According to Wiltshire, the officer then added, 'Don't cause any more bother Gerry, just take your money plus 10 per cent.' It was a clear offer of a bribe. Wiltshire replied, 'Who's put you up to this?'

Minutes afterwards Bain called Wiltshire to one side. According to Bain, the same officer had just threatened him, telling him to lay off the Garner inquiry. Furthermore, a second officer, a Detective Chief Inspector, had said that if there was any more trouble from Albany, Wiltshire would be pushed under a train.

The following month, March 1986, at the London Tara Hotel, Charles Flynn made the final arrangements on a kilo price for the cocaine. Garner was going to need his money in Hollywood now. Once again Smith called Peter Davy and told him he had sent two associates to Davy's house in Los Angeles.

In true Hollywood style Smith told Davy that if he looked out of his window he would see the two 'associates' outside. Davy looked; there were indeed two men. Davy panicked and called his associate for help. He told Davy to get Smith's men down to his office for a meeting. By then, he said, he would have guns and other back-up.

According to Davy he was about to approach the two men waiting outside when officers from the Los Angeles Police Department arrived. Davy's neighbour had apparently seen the men jumping over his garden fence. With the police present there was no trouble and the two English visitors agreed to meet Davy later that day. When they met up, Davy's associate was adamant. He told the couriers that the only way the money was going back to London was if Garner came to collect it himself.

Ten months later, that's exactly what Garner did. But when he arrived in Los Angeles there was a nasty surprise awaiting him. The $1,262,687.15 had completely disappeared.

17 · THE TULLEVERE TAPES

ROY WHITEHORNE WAS KEPT busy throughout the summer months of 1986. Into Brasilliance, his Fort Lauderdale jeweller's shop, came a steady stream of phone calls and visitors. As he was to tell Special Agents Minto and Breece later, 'These visits gave me considerable fears for my safety.' The callers were all Latin American and they all asked the same question: Where was Charles Flynn?

According to Whitehorne, in one of his secretly taped conversations with the wired-up Jimmy Tullevere, Flynn had refused to tell his Colombian suppliers about his movements. 'He didn't even tell them he was in London. They thought he was dealing in New York! Why should he tell them what country he's in? That way, nobody knows.'

The Colombian cocaine barons took a different view. They wanted new markets and they wanted to know who the big distributors were for their own future use. The only way they could find out was by following their sharp-end smugglers; men like Flynn. And of course there remained the ticklish question of what had happened to the hundreds of kilos of cocaine they had 'lent' to the engaging smuggler from Fort Lauderdale?

Another visitor to Whitehorne's store that summer was 'George', who had been seeking Flynn in Panama on the eve of the *Aquilon*'s voyage to England. According to Whitehorne,

'George' was desperate to find Charles as his family were being held hostage in Colombia at the time. 'George' had entrusted Flynn with $6 million worth of cocaine which he too had obtained on credit.

When Whitehorne finally heard from Flynn in London, he pleaded with him to get the Colombians off his back. 'Charles assured me that the pressure from Colombian families in Miami would cease,' he said. It did.

Throughout these months Whitehorne was also getting 'an awful lot of calls' from London. 'Sometimes from Mark Garner and possibly on one occasion from Roy Garner.' The contents of all these calls were passed on in considerable detail by the unsuspecting Whitehorne in his many conversations with Tullevere. In the Florida Department of Law Enforcement offices off South Cypress Road in Pompano Beach, Special Agents Minto and Breece went over each new tape, painstakingly extracting every scrap of information to help them piece together the jigsaw of the cocaine conspiracy.

By the summer of 1986 Detective Superintendent Lundy had bounced back to work at the heart of Scotland Yard. The previous year Commander Phil Corbett, head of Criminal Intelligence, had brought Lundy back from divisional CID in West London. Lundy was now one of a number of intelligence gathering officers drafted on to the Special Operations Task Force, formed to trace the £26 million of gold bullion stolen from the Brinks-Mat security warehouse at Heathrow in 1983. It was Britain's biggest ever robbery. Embarrassingly, the Yard had made little progress.

Lundy was now at the top of the integrated intelligence system. He had access to the best and most sensitive information in the Yard files. Coincidentally, the Yard re-organised the way it handled the informants system. In a bid to stamp out corruption it ruled that every informant should have a designated 'handler'. Lundy became Garner's handler. Corbett became their supervisor.

The Task Force, and its new recruit Tony Lundy, had moved their sights on from recovering the gold. They guessed that most of the ingots had been sold and their mission was to discover how the money had been laundered and seize the assets.

According to Scotland Yard files, once Lundy joined the Task Force they soon discovered the route of the laundered Brinks-Mat money. In secret Yard reports Lundy claimed that the source of this information was Roy Garner, who had been sitting in jail since his conviction for the VAT swindle.

Garner had been moved from Ford open prison in Sussex after he had been discovered bribing a prison officer. But, as always, he was looked after and, far from being punished by banishment to a stinking Victorian prison like other convicts, he was re-housed at the pleasant new Wayland prison in Norfolk.

Once Garner was ensconced in Wayland the visits from Lundy began. They had to be kept secret from other prisoners. Pretending to be going to hospital, Garner was taken to a nearby police station where Lundy was waiting. They met twice during March 1985 and each time Lundy claimed that Garner had given him important information. They had a further meeting in April. Before long Lundy — sometimes accompanied by Commander Corbett — was spending long periods in Florida and the Caribbean in pursuit of the missing millions.

Lundy later described Garner's information about the money-laundering in this way: 'In 1985 he started telling me things which triggered off my visit to Florida. He was directly responsible for it.' He added, 'It was a matter which became the biggest armed robbery ever.' He was referring to Brinks-Mat.

The truth is that the money-laundering route was discovered through surveillance on a long-established London armed robber who from the beginning of the Brinks-Mat investigation was a prime suspect. He is a man we will call 'Bond'. This is not his real name. A month after the robbery he flew to Miami with an Isle of Man money-launderer named Patrick Diamond. Together they met a Miami lawyer who worked with Diamond. They put together a series of property deals that would profitably hide some of Bond's share of the robbery. Bond then went off to live in Spain, but before leaving Florida he and Diamond met a drugs smuggler and professional killer named Scott Erico.

The detectives guessed that Diamond was fronting for Bond's money but they needed more evidence before they could move.

A year later Diamond was caught in London with a small amount of cocaine and jailed for eight months. Scott Erico was then arrested at Heathrow in transit from the US on his way to Spain to see Bond. He was interrogated by Lundy and then held for extradition to the US where he was wanted for murder.

Erico volunteered to help the police and told Lundy that Patrick Diamond had opened bank accounts and formed companies for himself and Bond. Confronted with the evidence Diamond cracked. He admitted his role in the Brinks-Mat laundering and also led Lundy to another money-laundering ring based in the British Virgin Islands. It was a major success for the Yard after all the disappointments in the Brinks-Mat case but the initial leads all came from observations on Erico and Diamond. For much of the money-laundering investigation in the Caribbean, Lundy based himself in Fort Lauderdale.

When Detective Sergeant Bain had visited Minto and Breece in Florida in August 1986 the detectives worked out a secure way to get copies of the Tullevere tapes safely back to England. Every couple of weeks Breece would take a package of tapes and make the hour-long drive down to Miami Airport. Here he would meet up with a British Airways Security officer who would get one of their flight crew to carry the package on the next flight out to London. Breece would call Bain in London with the flight details and the detective drove down the M4 to Heathrow Airport, collected the tapes and then stored them carefully under lock and key at Scotland Yard.

Special Agent Mike Breece sat in his Pompano Beach office packing up the latest selection of tapes. He called British Airways at Miami to warn them that he would be making another delivery in a couple of days. On Wednesday 17 September 1986 the airline called him back. Did he know that there was a Scotland Yard officer booked on the Friday evening flight to London? Why didn't Breece save himself the journey to Miami and give the tapes to the Scotland Yard officer staying just a few blocks away from Breece's office?

Breece was given the name and a hotel number. According to British Airways, the Scotland Yard officer was called Tony Lundy. Breece called Lundy and introduced himself. He explained that he had some tapes to send to a Detective Sergeant Bain at Scotland Yard. Would Lundy be kind enough to carry them back with him when he returned to England? Lundy was most obliging. Certainly he would do Breece the small favour that he asked.

Arrangements were made for Breece to drop by with the Tullevere tapes. Breece then called Bain at Scotland Yard to tell him about the arrangement with Lundy. Bain could not believe what he heard. He exploded down the phone, telling Breece that on no account must Lundy get hold of the Tullevere tapes.

They agreed that Breece was to call Lundy back and explain that he had discovered that the tapes Bain wanted were not connected with official police business. Bain was active in the International Police Association and he would tell Lundy that they were IPA tapes. This was the story Breece told Lundy when he called him back later. Breece made as good a job of the cover story as he could.

'I told Lundy that I was furious with Bain, that he had no right to use FDLE resources on private matters and that I would now send the tapes through the regular mail.' What's more, he told Lundy, he would be sending Bain a bill for the postage! It was all pretty desperate stuff and Tony Lundy had not been a detective for 24 years for nothing. According to Breece, Lundy's immediate comment was, 'Has Gordon Bain put you up to this?' Breece dissembled and ended the call. Lundy did not get the tapes. But, inevitably, he had learned a lot of extremely confidential information.

As a result of his unexpected talk with special agent Breece, Lundy had stumbled on the secret cocaine investigation. He now knew that tapes – almost certainly covert surveillance tapes – were being sent from detectives in Pompano Beach, Garner's US base, to Sergeant Bain at Scotland Yard.

It was common knowledge that Bain had singlemindedly dedicated himself to nailing Garner. Lundy also knew of Garner's previous involvement with cocaine in the early 1980s and that the criminal was now operating in the cocaine dealing capital of the world. Furthermore Lundy had learned that whatever information was on those tapes, the FDLE had dissembled to keep it from him.

Later Lundy was to tell a different story about the Tullevere tapes. He claimed he could not remember who had contacted him in Florida. He did recall however that there had been only one telephone call. He had simply been asked to deliver a package to London. He claimed that he had never known the contents of the package and certainly not that there were tapes in it.

Anyone who contemplates carrying a mystery package on a

trans-Atlantic flight without finding out exactly what the contents are would appear remarkably gullible. The concept of any half competent detective doing this, let alone one of Lundy's rank and experience, simply beggars belief. For years travellers between America and the UK have been met at airport check-in desks with the familiar questions 'Have you packed all your own luggage? Has anyone given you a package to carry?'

Whatever Lundy may or may not have been able to recall about the row over the Tullevere tapes, it is a matter of record that within 16 days of his return to Scotland Yard on 22 September, someone told the cocaine conspirators that they were under investigation.

Over the previous three weeks Flynn had started to shift the mountain of cocaine sitting in Roebuck House, Victoria. The cocaine was broken down into parcels of around 5 kilos and taken to a Northern Line tube station. At mid-day Flynn or one of his American couriers, Brian Van der Breen or Lee Bryan, would wait outside the station holding a yellow US aviation magazine called *Trade-A-Plane* for identification. One of Garner's associates would drive by, pick up the courier, take the bag of cocaine and drop the man off at the next tube station down the line.

To collect his payment Flynn would wait outside a well-known London location, like Regents Park or Victoria Station. On one occasion the money was in a plastic shopping bag with spaghetti packets covering it. In the first three weeks of distribution Flynn was paid about £350,000. As the distribution went on and the money flowed in Flynn made payments to the London representative of the Colombian cartel. One day, outside the Tara Hotel, Flynn handed over $2,300,000 in plastic carrier bags.

Flynn was due to meet one of Garner's team in early October to collect payment for his latest deliveries of cocaine. But no one turned up. When Flynn called the contact number he had for such eventualities, he was told that nobody could help him. According to Flynn, he then did a little detective work of his own. First he traced the address of that contact number. Then, dressing himself in a dark suit and white and black striped shirt 'to look a little bit sinister' he took a cab.

The man he met at the address remembers, 'I received a visit from what I would describe as an unsavoury gentleman, of heavy build, bald with short side-hair and a beard, wearing black shoes, black socks, black trousers and as far as I can recall a check jacket. He walked straight into the house and said he was owed £1 million. Although he made no threats, I was very uncomfortable in his presence.'

The international phone lines hummed at the news that Garner's operation had ground to a halt. As usual it was Whitehorne in his Fort Lauderdale shop who was at the centre of the calls. 'I was aware, from a call from Charles, that Garner's team had missed a London meeting,' he told Operation Redskin investigators. Around 8 October Whitehorne was called from London and told that 'they had a problem with Customs'. Whitehorne was also told that they were not sure if the problem was with Garner's team 'or with Charles and the boat'.

That was it: the secret investigation was blown. As each day passed the news became worse — and more specific. Whitehorne's revelations continued, 'Charles phoned and advised me to stay off my phone as the problems were coming from my phone. The same day a friend of Garner's phoned and told me the exact same message.' The gang's inside information was almost entirely accurate. They knew that their 'problem' was inside Whitehorne's shop. All they had wrong was that it was Whitehorne's mouth — and not his phone — that was taped.

Whitehorne told Tullevere about this worrying development. He said he thought that his telephone was tapped or even that his shop was being bugged. In a scene of pure irony Whitehorne asked Tullevere if he could trace the source of the leak! This greatly appealed to Tullevere's sense of humour. With his radio microphone faithfully picking up every word, Tullevere told an increasingly agitated Whitehorne, 'Now you're getting paranoid Roy, you're getting paranoid!'

Minto and Breece, listening to the Tullevere tapes, quickly learnt that their investigation was no longer secret. Whitehorne's language to Tullevere was colourful. 'Charles calls and says keep off your fucking phone. All the aggravation is coming from your fucking end. I said bullshit. Now I think there may be a problem because I've had all these fucking calls coming in from cunts in Colombia and idiots in Panama. Maybe somebody's twigged those fucking phone calls.'

Whitehorne and the rest of the conspirators also knew that their problem was coming from tape recordings. 'It might be a Federal tap because if it's a Federal tap then they record it on to a tape. Then they listen to it for anything that might be useful. Can you go and find out for me? Because I've just got to find out.'

As Minto and Breece listened further to the tape recording of Whitehorne's conversation with Tullevere, they were shaken to discover the apparent source of the leak to the conspirators. Whitehorne continued: 'They heard from this fucking guy at Scotland Yard that Charles had got some problems.'

'You've got a guy at Scotland Yard?'

'Yes, oh yes . . . '

'Come on, that's like getting a fucking FBI agent here. They're tough to get up.'

'Oh yes they have, they've had him for a long time . . . When he fucked off he told him that Roy Garner . . . '

'You're knocking my whole fucking image of Scotland Yard.'

'They've got the guy paid off.'

18 · IN THE HEART OF THE YARD

GARNER WAS IN A MESS. The authorities were on to the cocaine conspiracy.

On 13 October he sent an envoy to meet with Chrastny in one of the European capital cities. 'He told me about difficulties he was being informed about by his contact in the Yard that had arisen in the States through wire taps . . . and that he didn't dare to proceed for the time being with further business transactions with me. He also told me that he was already sorting things out and was going to introduce me to another gentleman who was going to handle things in the future.'

That evening, over dinner, Flynn was introduced to his new British partners. Both men were called Mick. It was a social occasion and business was not discussed that night. The following day the four men met again in a park and this time they got down to the serious business of cocaine distribution. As darkness fell they went on haggling in a nearby winebar.

Flynn claims that he knew one of the two Micks already. This was Mickey Green. Green had been one of the first operators to see the simple beauty of the gold Krugerrand swindle and he had stolen nearly £6 million from the taxpayers. Although he had the stake money to buy into Flynn's cocaine operation, Green had a problem. His Krugerrand adventure had resulted in a British warrant for his arrest and obliged him to go into exile on Spain's notorious Costa del Crime. So it was the second 'Mick' who had to be the new day-to-day London contact.

According to Chrastny, this man was 'about forty-eight years old, greyish hair, cockney accent and a very distinguished scar on his neck. It looked to me like it could have been a gunshot injury. There was some tissue missing.' The second Mick had been wounded in a South London gangland shooting war ten years earlier. He was lucky to escape; his brother had been shot dead. Flynn was particularly impressed that his new contact 'was a very serious man, since two of the people involved in the shooting have found an untimely end and in the meanwhile he is working on the others.'

Chrastny's new friend with the gunshot wound on the neck was Micky Henessey, a member of one of London's prominent gangland families. A year after Garner was charged with the cocaine conspiracy Operation Redskin caught up with Henessey and charged him with importing and distributing the drug. But then the magistrates at the Guildhall were swayed by a brilliant performance on the part of his barrister and, on 11 October 1988, they let him go. Hugh Donagher, Operation Redskin's senior investigator, stormed from the court when the Magistrates found that Henessey had no case to answer.

Henessey looked as shocked as Donagher as he left the court clutching a white plastic bag containing his belongings. Henessey's exit went completely unnoticed by the ranks of press photographers waiting for the outcome of a case in an adjoining court. In the period that Henessey was Chrastny's London contact, he shifted some 300 kilos of cocaine on to the streets of Britain. Today, his whereabouts are unknown.

By the second half of October 1986 Roy Garner had managed to sever his links with the London end of the cocaine conspiracy. Flynn's new line of distribution through Micky Henessey was working well. From his cell in Wayland prison Roy Garner, aware that the investigation into the cocaine conspiracy was under way, now moved to distance himself completely from any involvement in the crime. The time had come for Garner to change sides. Out went the gangster and in came Scotland Yard's best ever informant.

Garner had discovered that Granada TV's *World in Action* series was making a programme about him. While out of prison on home leave he had seen a film crew outside his North London mansion. Garner had watched them on the remote-controlled video camera mounted outside the family home. He had also heard that in the previous days the crew had been filming at Holborn Stud Farm where Garner kept his trotting horses, and at the house in Finchley where his other wife, Phyllis Garner, was living with their daughter.

The idea of a television programme about Garner and his relationship with Lundy was first raised in 1984 by two of the authors of this book who were then working for the BBC. In early 1985 a sixty-minute documentary called 'The Untouchable' was made for the *Brass Tacks* series. The research and filming were going well, until the journalists contacted the Yard for comment.

The Yard's assault on the BBC film makes a mockery of its claims to be open with the media. It launched its attack the moment it learned of the BBC project. The first target was Harry Clement, who had been tracked down in retirement by BBC journalists and had told them about the unsuccessful efforts of Operation Albany. Commander Phil Corbett, head of the Yard's Criminal Intelligence branch, was dispatched in a chauffeur driven car to Clement's remote farmhouse in North Devon. He quizzed Clement about what he had told the BBC. Clement's reply was robust: back at the Yard were all the Albany and Stagg files. 'Go and look at the dockets,' said Clement, 'all you need to know is there.' He was of course referring to the Steventon memo.

That was not what the Yard wanted to hear. The last thing it needed to be reminded of was the time-bomb it was sitting on. Clement declined to go into detail about what he had said to the journalists. A few weeks later Clement heard from friends at the Yard about the whispering campaign against him. The word was being spread about that he had gone mad and was leaking information that would damage the system for protecting informants. Clement was deeply hurt by these slurs. He had won his bravery awards the hard way and his retirement was marred by considerable pain from an old back injury. The officers maligning him were ambitious desk drivers. Clement made his own inquiries at the local telephone exchange and became convinced that his phone was being tapped.

After Corbett's visit to Devon the Yard felt confident that the Steventon memo had not yet reached the journalists. But there were other officers who might have a copy. Whoever they were, they must be prevented from leaking it. One of the most senior officers at the Yard then wrote a private letter to the office of the Director of Public Prosecutions; could Clement be prosecuted under the Official Secrets Act? The request was brusquely denied. The fact remains that the Yard was desperate enough to try to drag Clement through the courts in order to protect Lundy and Garner.

The next stage of the attack was to draft a surveillance squad on to one of the BBC journalists. For two months the squad photographed his home and every person he met. They suspected he was meeting serving officers who were leaking information about the scandal. They were unsuccessful. It is likely that his phone was tapped as well.

Stories attacking the film were planted in the *Daily Mirror* and in *Private Eye* and a senior Home Office civil servant was recruited to help 'nobble' the BBC. At a routine meeting between the Government department and Corporation managers a BBC executive was taken aside and warned that some of the *Brass Tacks* witnesses were unreliable. How the Home Office had found out who those witnesses were was not disclosed.

To drive the message home Assistant Commissioner Dellow wrote to the Director General of the BBC: 'I am writing personally and confidentially in connection with a programme I understand the BBC intends transmitting as part of the "Brass Tacks" series. The programme, I am led to believe, will deal with issues relating to police handling of informers and may allege incompetency and/or corruption.'

After making his case against the showing of any such programme Dellow then issued a warning. 'There has already been some public discussion of varying depth and accuracy of the matters raised. However, we have never before had prior knowledge of such disclosures and in any case feel that there has now been reached a point in the process of attrition where we should make a stand.'

Dellow concluded with the usual Scotland Yard plea about the best place for any allegations of corruption that might have come to the attention of journalists. 'I would suggest that public interest would be best served by immediate report of the allegations to the Commissioner . . . if you feel a meeting with you to discuss the issues before transmission would help I am more than willing to make myself available.'

Dellow's efforts were successful. The BBC's Assistant Director General, Alan Protheroe, decided that 'The Untouchable' was not to be transmitted. He relied on an opinion from the BBC solicitors, who believed that there were insuperable problems with the programme.

The *Brass Tacks* team went outside the BBC legal department and sought leading counsel's opinion. Some script changes were suggested and the programme was pronounced safe to transmit. The BBC hierarchy refused to budge.

More changes were made and eventually the BBC's senior solicitor advised, 'In the revised format the libel and other legal risks associated with this project have been reduced to an acceptable level having regard to the importance of the issues which the programme has raised. Ultimately it is an editorial decision whether the importance of the issues raised justifies the libel and contempt risks referred to above. My own view, for what it is worth, is that it does.'

The opinion of the BBC's chief solicitor came too late to prevent Protheroe writing to the *Guardian* that 'This programme will not be transmitted because of insoluble legal difficulties not — as you suggest — following representations from Scotland Yard. The issues raised by *Brass Tacks* are of great importance: they will be the subject of a future programme.'

Protheroe was correct; the issues were of great importance and there would be a future programme, but it would not be screened by the BBC. By October 1986, the journalists who had made 'The Untouchable' for *Brass Tacks* had left the BBC and joined Granada TV, who commissioned the remaking of the programme for the *World In Action* documentary series. It was ready for transmission on Monday 3 November.

The fact that 'The Untouchable' was up and running again offered Garner the perfect opportunity to distance himself from the cocaine plot. From prison, Garner called the Yard and demanded an urgent meeting. On the afternoon of 30 October the convict was met at the Yard by DAC Worth and his Staff Officer,

Guardian, 15 Oct 1985

Guardian, 16 Oct 1985

"I would be at home watching television but all the programmes worth seeing keep being cancelled."

DCS Roy Ramm. Unknown to Garner, the two policemen were secretly tape-recording the meeting. First, they had to put up with a tirade of abuse from the criminal.

'You're going to have to put up with ten minutes waffling from me first because I'm just black and blue over you people,' Garner exploded. 'I'm not up to here, I'm up to here with it!'

With that off his chest, Garner explained the urgency of his call the previous day. He told the two officers that he feared another attempt was being made to turn him into a television star. 'Because you stopped "Brass Tacks", Granada has taken it up.' With his history of informing, said Garner, 'I'll be the first to go if that television comes out.'

He then bluntly threatened the two officers. 'If you want a scandal it'll come if me or my family is hurt and if this television programme goes on.'

Having taken the stick to the dogs, Garner gave them a glimpse of the rabbit. 'Now . . . I'm too intelligent to threaten because I mean please don't . . . I'm here to negotiate. But please can I leave here letting you know how serious it all is.'

Worth's only recorded comment to this is, 'Mmmm'.

Garner proceeded to show more of the rabbit. '710 kilos of cocaine was brought into this country in July of this year. Now if that ain't a national problem to ya God knows what is . . . You've got to believe me, I only knew about this Tuesday of this week when Mr Somebody ran off with my money and I started to make deep, firm inquiries . . . Now you ain't ever going to catch this firm they've got too much money for ya, they've got too much coming for ya, and now they're established.'

Garner went on to explain in great detail how the cocaine was wrapped, how it was transported, where on the boat it was concealed, and how it would be distributed using black London taxis. He also stated that he knew the man behind it all. According to Garner, the man's name was 'Jan'.

He then gave a remarkable explanation of how he knew all this without being involved himself. 'Now they wanted to open up this in France, Belgium, 'olland, all this you know . . . now the best man at the time must have looked like me for them.'

The reason that Garner had been offered the distribution rights for the largest amount of cocaine this country has ever seen was apparently the great impression his criminal exploits had made on 'Jan'.

'Jan came across here prior to my trial. 'e reads that I'm capable of swindling the VAT man out of £3 million. He knows what stock I've got in America . . . when they decide to go to work in London what better than a horsy racing man with probably one of the best clubs in London, pound for pound. I mean, my club earns more than Stringfellows.'

Now the rabbit was really racing and Garner sprung the trap. 'I want Granada off my back and in return 710 kilos will be arriving here, I know how it's coming, I know approximately when it will come, and I would like to deal for it . . . One thing Mr Worth, I know I'm political, I know if you're seen to be helping me too much you're gonna have the press and I don't want to give you a problem, but I don't think I've had a crack of the whip from this building. Is there a way of putting it right?'

Garner also asked if Worth could stop Granada by threatening to use the Official Secrets Act.

'If it is "World In Action",' replied Worth, 'then they'll take a lot of stopping. Certainly the Official Secrets Act won't do it.'

His Staff Officer, Roy Ramm, agreed. 'They are probably the

top documentary firm in the country, they're not Mickey Mouse. I mean they do big stuff.'

'What you're saying,' mused Worth, closing on the rabbit, 'is that if we can stop this programme . . . you want to give us information concerning another 710 kilos of cocaine, that's right?'

'Yes, yes,' replied Garner, 'it's a specific 700 because the compartment it fits in holds it nicely.'

Worth pondered on the problem of stopping the imminent *World In Action* transmission. 'I don't have the sort of power to stop the programme,' he said. 'They are a very high-grade investigative set-up, "World In Action".'

Worth told Garner that he was pessimistic but said he would talk to his boss, Assistant Commissioner John Dellow. 'We'll give it our best shot.'

'What is exercising my mind,' said Staff Officer Ramm, belatedly waking up to Garner's earlier threat 'is that you said that you covered yourself and if we wanted a scandal . . . '

'Do you really mean me to say it?' Garner interrupted. 'Well, if it's a choice between my family suffering any more or this building, who's it going to be?'

Ramm's only recorded comment at this repeated threat is also 'Mmm'.

''ow could anybody as good as me be dumped?' continued Garner, warming to his theme. 'Let's face it, grasses get padded cells with coloured television, carpet and visits from their old woman. I mean, what did I get, what did you give me? You just absolutely threw me to the wolves. And I don't believe you stopped "Brass Tacks" for me. You stopped "Brass Tacks" for Lundy.'

'I think,' murmured, DAC Worth 'we stopped "Brass Tacks" for the danger coming out of it.'

'For yourself,' said Garner. And again he returned to the cocaine conspiracy. Garner revealed, quite brazenly, that he was aware the crime was under investigation.

'Now, who's your biggest man with cocaine in this building?' he asked. There was no response from the two policemen.

Garner persevered. 'Right, get 'old of the biggest man and 'e will inform you that he has received information that a massive load of cocaine is on its way . . . You're sitting here and saying nothing and I'm doing all the talking, 20, 30 per cent of what I've told you, you already know.'

Garner was very well informed. Customs' Operation Redskin had indeed been up and running for over two months by this stage. The Yard's own Operation Distant Drum, acting as liaison between Customs, the Yard, the Florida Department of Law Enforcement and the German BKA had been set up at the same time.

Yet Ramm and Worth appear to have acted as if they were ignorant of all this. It was Worth himself who had authorised Bain's visit to Florida that August and so would be aware of the operational arrangements set up on his return. He had to know that Customs and Excise were leading the investigation, yet no mention of Garner's visit to the Yard that day, let alone what was said, was passed on to the Operation Redskin investigators. Had not Sergeant Bain spotted Garner at the Yard that afternoon, Operation Redskin might never have known.

The meeting was drawing to a close. As he readied himself to leave, Garner asked Staff Officer Ramm if he had ever tried cocaine. Ramm replied stiffly that he hadn't.

'Ain't bad,' said Garner, 'try it. I'll be on it I should think for the next two years, killing the pain.' He then asked if the two senior officers could arrange a back way for him to get out of the Yard.

'You'll piss yourself with laughter,' Ramm told Garner after he'd come off the phone making the arrangements for Garner's exit. 'The door you would have been going out of would have been the recruiting branch and I've got to tell you, we're not going to have you at any price!'

Scotland Yard did do what Garner asked of it. On the following afternoon, Granada TV received a letter from Assistant Commissioner John Dellow, similar to the one he had sent the BBC the previous year, asking the company to think carefully before transmitting its *World in Action* programme.

Three days later the updated version of 'The Untouchable' opened with secretly shot pictures of Garner delivering Krugerrands to Hatton Garden bullion dealers. The script began: 'This man is Roy Garner. Here he is stealing £2 million. That's all in a day's work for Roy Garner because, according to the Metropolitan Police, he's one of the biggest criminals in London. But Garner has led a charmed life. In the last 20 years he's never picked up a serious conviction from the Met. What he has picked up, on the Met's recommendation, is nearly a quarter of a million pounds in rewards for informing on his fellow criminals.'

Now, after years of frustration, the story was being told. Nearly eight million viewers heard retired Detective Superintendent Gerry Wiltshire, the second head of Operation Albany, describe Garner as 'The organiser, the overlord of serious crime in London today'. It was a title that would stick. Wiltshire's predecessor, Harry Clement, followed with the story of the obstruction of Albany. Garner was disclosed as Lundy's informant and the programme revealed Lundy's 1981 letter to Powis backing Garner for the £300,000 Silver Bullion reward. It also revealed the arrangement for the head of detectives and the criminal to meet, even while Albany was at its height.

A chunk of Steventon's secret memo suggesting Lundy was corrupt was quoted and then the programme moved on to Lundy's curious evidence on behalf of gunman Lennie Gibson at the Old Bailey. Wiltshire appeared again and was asked if the Yard had tried hard enough to claw back the money Garner had hidden in America. He replied, tartly: 'Scotland Yard hasn't tried at all. It's our team that has been trying.'

Then Wiltshire revealed the bribe offered to him by a senior Yard detective to halt the hunt for Garner's assets overseas — and the death threat if he did not. He was asked, 'Did you take this death threat seriously?' He replied, 'I most certainly did, I've been threatened before, of course, but when it comes from a senior police officer you take it seriously.' Wiltshire went on to claim that the Yard had done nothing more than give the senior detective 'a ticking off' for the death threat.

The programme ended with the revelation that Garner was being put forward as the man responsible for 'grassing' on the £26 million Brinks-Mat money-laundering. The credits rolled and, at last, the story was in the public domain. Coincidentally, Granada TV's Chairman, Sir Denis Forman, appeared on a BBC discussion programme later that night and was asked about attempts to stop the programme. He replied, 'You can't be leant on. You must not be leant on.'

The Yard press office, bombarded with late-night queries from the media, attempted to kill the story with a 'business as usual' statement. The spokesman claimed, 'No evidence has ever been revealed to indicate any Metropolitan police officers acted improperly.' The allegation that Garner had informed on the missing Brinks-Mat millions was dismissed as 'utterly false, as were many of the other alleged facts contained in the programme'.

But the story was out of control. Within an hour of the screening Labour MPs Clive Soley and Chris Smith put down an Early Day Motion naming Lundy as corrupt and calling for an independent inquiry. It was published too late for the next day's papers but that did not matter. There was enough to report already: nearly every national newspaper carried stories of the death threat to Wiltshire.

The debate about how to respond to the disclosures raged through the night and into the following Tuesday on the Command floor at the Yard. Simultaneously, members of the Police Complaints Authority at their offices off Whitehall were becoming restless and there was talk of contacting the Yard to insist on an outside inquiry. Soon after lunch a call came through to say that Commissioner Kenneth Newman had appointed the South Yorkshire Police to investigate the *World in Action* allegations.

An hour later MP Clive Soley was on his feet in the House of Commons. The Speaker refused his call for an emergency debate on the corruption allegations. No one in the press gallery noticed the significance of Soley's comment that 'It has been suggested to me that a serious drugs offence has already been partly started but that it is not being dealt with in the way in which it ought to be dealt with.' It appeared that one of the Opposition's front bench spokesmen knew more than the leadership of the Yard about Garner's £100 million cocaine deal.

Lundy was still in the Caribbean and three days passed before his response to 'The Untouchable' was telexed to the press. He made no attempt to answer the allegations. Instead, he went on the attack. 'The fact that members of Parliament can irresponsibly make unsubstantiated general allegations that I am corrupt while hiding behind Parliamentary privilege is absolutely disgusting . . . the latest series of allegations have taken different and sinister lines of attack.'

Lundy claimed to be the victim of 'malicious and unfounded allegations which have been investigated and I have been fully exonerated.' He went on to claim, 'I have no doubt that numerous criminals backed up by certain sections of the media are determined to discredit me and thus open the floodgates from prison.'

No doubt Lundy's eccentric assertions were noted by South Yorkshire Chief Constable Peter Wright as he arrived in London to begin his inquiries. He and his team were given office space on the sixth floor of Wellington House, a Met administration block in Buckingham Gate near the Palace. Before long nearly 20 detectives were based there. Initially they believed they would be finished within three months. It would be more than a year before they returned to their families in Sheffield, Barnsley and Rotherham. Their inquiry was to be the third most expensive in the short history of the Police Complaints Authority. The cost was borne by the London ratepayers.

Early on in their inquiries they made a curious request to Granada Television. Some years before, *World in Action* had made a programme about the huge 'Operation Countryman' inquiries into corruption in the Met. Countryman had of course been dogged with claims of obstruction from the Met. Could the South Yorkshire police please have a copy? The request was granted.

The pressure on Lundy piled up. A month later, in December 1986, he appeared as a witness in a cocaine trial at Southwark Crown Court. On the face of it the two defendants had no chance. They had been caught red-handed with two kilos of the drug. Eventually Lundy was called to give evidence and defence counsel Michael West was waiting for him. Lundy glared round the court, gripped the side of the box, threw his head back and prepared for combat. West slaughtered him. He produced the Steventon memo and asked, 'Is it not the case that you have split the Metropolitan police down the middle, between those who believe you are a successful officer and those who believe you are corrupt?'

Lundy lost his temper and launched a bitter attack on *World in Action* and two of the authors who were sitting on the press benches. He claimed that the media allegations were 'blatant and outright lies' and announced that legal action was in hand.

In a matter of minutes Lundy threw away both the prosecution case and what was left of his career as a detective. The jury took a short while to acquit the defendants and Lundy could never appear again as a prosecution witness. Now it was clear why the Yard had suppressed the Steventon memo.

Journalists and photographers gathered in the dark outside the court, waiting to interview Lundy. He walked across the terrace and when he reached the pavement the flash bulbs went off. Astonishingly, Lundy panicked and ran back into the building to emerge some minutes later from the underground car park slumped in the back of an unmarked police car. It was his last public appearance as a Scotland Yard officer.

On 5 January 1987 Garner flew to Los Angeles, not knowing that his US visa had been cancelled. He got as far as the immigration desk. There he encountered the bulky figure of Special Agent Felix Rocha of the Organised Crime and Racketeering section of the Los Angeles Strike Force, a division of the US Justice Department.

When asked about his business in America, Garner was uncharacteristically frank. He explained about the loss of the money handled by Peter Davy and his accomplices. He said he had come to 'try and sort this firm of lawyers out'. Garner then expressed astonishment that he was being interviewed. 'I was never told that my visa was going to be revoked although I checked with London policemen on two occasions.'

Surprised, Rocha inquired, 'Can you tell me the name of that London police officer?' Garner certainly could. 'Chief Superintendent Lundy'. That was the end of the interview on oath but Garner wanted to say more. Referring to Davy's business associate, he said that 'no plastic gangster' was going to keep his money. If Rocha would just give him an hour he could recover it. Garner assured Rocha that on his return to Britain he would get Lundy to call on his behalf because he had 'always co-operated with police in the past'. Unimpressed, Rocha escorted Garner on to the next plane to London. It was the start of what was to be a rotten year for the gangster.

19 · ON THE RUN

THE AMERICAN EMBASSY in London's Grosvenor Square handles over half a million applications for visas and passports every year. Around mid-morning on 20 November 1986, Nelda Green was working her way through the day's pile of paperwork when she came to a passport renewal application in the name of Charles Albert Flynn. Cross-checking 'Flynn' with files in Washington, she discovered that the passport was 'flagged'; there could be no renewal without reference to higher authority. The application form, along with two passport pictures, had been brought into Grosvenor Square by a woman called Tabitha Thomas. Later, the investigators discovered that Thomas was the Chrastny family nanny, in charge of 'little Charles', their seven-year-old son. Nelda Green called Thomas to the counter.

'I asked her where Mr Flynn was staying, and she said the Tara Hotel.' Nelda Green played for time. She told Thomas that to renew the passport Mr Flynn would have to come to the Embassy in person. Green gave Thomas her phone number and asked that Flynn make contact. Later that afternoon Nelda Green took a call from Charles Flynn. 'He spoke with a slight foreign accent, not American or British. He asked me what the problem was with his passport.' She told Flynn there was no problem, it was just that the Embassy procedure required him to call into Grosvenor Square to collect his new passport.

Flynn said he would be in the following afternoon. Nelda Green reported this to the resident FBI man at the Embassy who liaises with the British authorities.

The following morning the Embassy and the Tara Hotel were staked out by Customs officers, backed up by police sharpshooters. They waited patiently for their quarry, but Chrastny was not taking any risks. All they were left with at the end of the day was Flynn's old passport. The Redskin team checked it carefully and towards the back, among the entry and exit stamps, were Panamanian entries for a boat called the *Aquilon*.

Customs and Excise keeps records of all vessels docking in British waters. Within hours they had located the boat. She was berthed at the Hamble Marina near Southampton. A Customs team watched for 24 hours and then quietly boarded the former North Sea pilot vessel. They searched her from stem to stern and eventually found what they were looking for. Inside her fuel tanks were the specially built compartments which had been installed in Eggert Kronby's Puntarenas boatyard and which three months earlier had held 392 kilos of cocaine.

Special Agent Mike Minto rang London to pass on the news — the BKA in Wiesbaden had finally come up with the true identity of 'Charles Albert Flynn'. For the first time in their long investigations the detectives on both sides of the Atlantic knew the real name of the man they were tracking. It was Nikolaus Maria Chrastny. They still did not know his whereabouts, but thought he was within striking distance of London. If he *was* in England, then he probably had with him most of the three-quarters of a ton of cocaine that Whitehorne had boasted about.

Chrastny was certainly moving the drugs fast. At the time of Minto's call he was busy reducing his stockpile with the help of his new distributors. Chrastny would meet Micky Henessey, his new contact, outside Baker Street tube station to deliver around 10 or 12 kilos of cocaine at a time. In return, Henessey handed over between £150,000 and £200,000. He always stuffed the notes into small hold-alls. On some days Chrastny would make two deliveries and relieve Henessey of more than £300,000 in cash.

The two criminals developed an admiration bordering on friendship. Henessey took Chrastny on guided tours of the

English countryside. On one occasion they went to look round Windsor, on another to Cambridge. Henessey was a lover of classical music, particularly Wagner. As they drove along the country lanes with the German masterpieces resounding from the car stereo, Henessey would muse on the pleasures of life and quote the odd few lines of Shakespeare.

In early November, Chrastny's new-found friend gave him a video tape. On it was recorded that month's *World In Action* programme about the Garner and Lundy relationship, called 'The Untouchable'. Operation Redskin investigators found this tape later in one of Chrastny's safehouses. He told them that when he watched it and discovered the true role of his former partner Garner 'It made me sick to my stomach'.

For safety's sake the cocaine was constantly moved to new addresses. They were all rented by a German woman using the name 'Mrs Kara' or 'Mrs Bauer', or sometimes 'Mrs Schreiber'. These were aliases for Chrastny's wife, Charlotte. The cocaine was stored at the flat in Roebuck House for some three months before Lee Bryan and Brian Van der Breen packed it into steel trunks and shifted the lot to a new home in Sloane Street. From here the gang moved the drugs to a house in Abbey Road. The house can be seen on the cover of the Beatles album of the same name.

Finally the drugs came to rest in a basement flat at 65 Harley Street. Here Van der Breen and another American he had recruited, Robert Cermack, were locked in with the cocaine. They only went out to make a delivery or to go to the local banks to swap the tide of incoming cash for larger denomination notes.

Meanwhile Charlotte Chrastny made her own forays into London with the drug money, but she didn't take it to the banks for conversion — she laundered it through Bond Street's exclusive boutiques. She bought clothes, furs, and jewellery. She spent thousands of pounds at a time, and it was always cash. She paid £1,050 for an Yves Saint Laurent skirt, £615 for a Gorgissima blouse and £1,879 for a Karl Lagerfeld skirt and dress. For one diamond necklace from jewellers Young, Stephen in the Burlington Arcade she handed over £132,250 in used notes. Apparently there was nothing unusual in such transactions. In one month alone Charlotte Chrastny spent over half a million pounds along Bond Street.

Her husband spent some of the money too. He was an avid collector of antique Japanese ceremonial swords. He paid £74,000 for 20 swords from dealers in the Essex Road and Kensington High Street.

Charlotte Chrastny had rented a second flat, at 69 Harley Street, for herself and her husband. It was conveniently situated overlooking number 65, which housed the cocaine. From the kitchen window, Charlotte could keep an eye on the safehouse through her binoculars.

But while Charlotte Chrastny was watching from her window, she herself was under observation. Once 'Flynn' had been identified as Chrastny, the German police staked out his and Charlotte's relatives in Southern Germany. Mail was opened, phones were tapped. Eventually, in May 1987, evidence came up which pointed to the happy home at 69 Harley Street where Chrastny, his wife and his young son Charles were living. Operation Redskin had the area staked out. Days later they took their first observation picture of Nikolaus and Charlotte Chrastny, disguised with hats and headscarves, as they came out of the flat.

The watchers waited for six weeks. Then, on Friday 19 June, they went in to arrest Chrastny. They had heard stories of his determination never to be taken alive and rumours that he had shot two policeman in the Caribbean who got too close to him. The decision was taken not to storm the flat, in case of a shoot-out. It would be safer to jump him on the pavement. No risks could be taken on a busy West End street and so the unarmed Customs officers were vastly outnumbered by the muscle from the Yard. Two 'troop carriers' from PT17, the Blue Berets marksmen based at Old Street, together with two attack dogs, stood by out of sight of Chrastny's Harley Street flat.

They waited patiently and at lunchtime he was spotted as he left the front door of number 69. The muscle went in. Chrastny was swept off his feet in a tidal wave of police officers and flattened to the pavement. He was shocked but kept his cool. The Redskin case officer, Bob Gray, asked him formally, 'Are you Nikolaus Chrastny?' The reply, in time-honoured fashion, was, 'I'm not saying anything.' He was told that he was being arrested in connection with cocaine smuggling.

Within an hour Chrastny was being questioned at the Customs Building in New Fetter Lane. By the end of the afternoon he had admitted that he was wanted for an armed robbery in Germany; that he knew who Roy Whitehorne was and that he knew the members of the *Aquilon* crew. He insisted that the £1 million in cash and jewellery found in his flat was the proceeds of the 1973 Munich jewel robbery; that he had nothing to do with drug-running, and that his dealings in Colombia were only in connection with diamonds. The interviews went on into the evening. Then he was left alone for the night with his thoughts.

Throughout the next morning Chrastny answered more questions but would not incriminate himself. However, he had been weighing up his options overnight. After a break for lunch he talked further but still denied any involvement in drugs. Then he began talking about Whitehorne and the Customs men told him that Whitehorne had been arrested in Florida, where he was confirming the information on the Tullevere tapes. Chrastny could not bluff much longer, the cocaine story was going to come out. Chrastny moved on to discuss the plight of his wife and young son.

Then the interrogators withdrew and both sides considered their positions. Seven hours later a senior Customs officer arrived to talk about a deal. They began negotiating at 8.15 that evening and within nine minutes the deal had been struck. Chrastny claimed he was fed up with life on the run and that if Customs would leave Charlotte out of any charges then he would co-operate. The Customs men knew that he must have a huge amount of cocaine hidden somewhere and it was their duty to find it. They agreed detailed conditions about living expenses and security for his family. Once that had been arranged, Chrastny told them what they wanted to hear.

He revealed that there were nearly 57 kilos of cocaine still stashed in suitcases under the stairs in the flat at 65 Harley Street. It was being guarded by Van der Breen and Cermack. He told them that the two Americans would surely have seen his arrest the previous day from their kitchen window and that the 'merchandise' would have been moved or destroyed by now. He added that at 10 am that day he should have met with his London distributor. This man owed him £1.2 million and missing the meeting could cause 'problems'.

While Chrastny claimed that he was willing to co-operate, he was still trying to control events; the longer he delayed talking about the cocaine, the more chance there was that it would be moved. The drugs still had a street value of more than £14 million. Perhaps something could be salvaged from his arrest. He clearly hoped that by the time he told Redskin about the second flat in Harley Street, the two Americans and the drugs would be gone. Unfortunately for Chrastny, when Customs Officers burst into the flat at 4 am the next day, the drugs and the American baby-sitters were still there.

Once he had started talking, Chrastny continued late into the night. There was one matter he was more than happy to reveal to his interrogators. Part of his deal with Garner was the protection he could provide from Scotland Yard. His British partner had assured him he had a friend high up in the Yard who could provide any information that they needed. The friend's name, he said, was Lundy.

Now it was Garner's turn to be arrested. A little after breakfast, two days later, the Redskin officers went to Cannon Lodge. Garner was outside the house walking his dog. He asked if their visit had anything to do with the drugs raid at Harley Street the previous weekend. Then he was cautioned and taken to New Fetter Lane for questioning. He was interviewed twice but refused to answer any questions. During these interviews Garner jabbed his finger at the tape-recorder indicating that he wanted it turned off.

When the machine stopped, he spoke. He told the investigators that he had never had any involvement with any drugs of any kind. He had never used drugs. He didn't know Flynn, Van der Breen, Cermack or Whitehorne. He repeatedly told the Customs investigators that he was innocent.

He then went on to deny that he had any foreign bank accounts or that he had ever travelled on false documents. He insisted that the only reason for his trips to America was his horse-breeding business and that he would be glad to help Customs and Excise with their investigation.

Well End is an exclusive little community set in the expensive Home Counties countryside near Shenley in Hertfordshire. On the Well End Road, past The Mop and Broom pub, the countryside opens out and there is a newly built five-bedroom mansion. It is set in nearly three-quarters of an acre of landscaped gardens and stands back from the road at the end of a gravel drive. The gate is guarded by an electronic lock and an intercom system. The view over the Green Belt countryside to the rear has been described as 'breathtaking'.

No expense has been spared in equipping the property. Each of the five bedrooms has its own en-suite bathroom and each set of taps is gold-plated. The same finish is applied to the taps in the downstairs cloakroom and even to the taps in the kitchen. The kitchen has three fridge units, two ovens and an array of electrical appliances. The rest of the ground floor includes the boiler room, boot room, utility room, TV room, dining room, snooker room with fitted bar and, finally, the reception room. A half-turn galleried staircase leads upstairs. To one side is a built-on double garage. The house is called 'The Laurels' and in early 1988, was valued at £800,000. It was designed by, and built for, Tony Lundy and his family.

Roy Garner had been detained in custody for just 16 days when Lundy's phone rang in The Laurels. It was nearly 7.30 on the morning of 9 July and he was about to leave for work. The caller was Garner's wife, June, and, according to Lundy, she was in a very distressed state. She had been told to pass on a message from Roy. She said, according to Lundy, that her husband 'needed some help with his situation'. June said that she didn't understand the message.

Lundy understood very clearly the kind of help Roy needed. He told June to tell her husband that 'certain information had been passed at a very senior level from Scotland Yard to senior personnel of the agency dealing with his case'. Lundy then went off to work at Scotland Yard. In accordance with his instructions now that the South Yorkshire police were investigating his relationship with Garner, he logged the call from June Garner. He did not dare do otherwise. It was more than likely that both his and Garner's phones were being monitored.

At 5.10 pm the following day Lundy was summoned to see Deputy Assistant Commissioner Peter Winship, who was in charge of discipline and internal investigations. Winship began by asking Lundy what he thought Garner meant by his request for help. Lundy said he believed he was referring to the meeting at Scotland Yard of 30 October 1986. This was the meeting at which Garner had revealed to Worth and Ramm the extent of his knowledge of the cocaine conspiracy and had offered to act as informant on the next run.

Winship asked Lundy what he thought he was doing telling Garner, the principal defendant in a forthcoming trial that Customs and Excise were aware of that meeting. Lundy insisted he had done nothing wrong. Winship reminded Lundy that he was under strict instruction to have no contact with Garner, and that if Garner contacted him he was under orders to say nothing.

Lundy persevered: he still couldn't see how he had done anything wrong. In his view he had merely passed on information that Garner's solicitors would be able to find out from Scotland Yard anyway. Winship replied that this was not a decision for Lundy to make, and that of all the Scotland Yard officers who might be called upon to make such a decision, Lundy was the one officer expressly forbidden from doing so.

Winship then outlined the gravity of the situation. He asked Lundy, did he not think that the information he had passed on to Garner the previous morning could be of considerable use to him? Garner was in prison, alone, facing charges which could result in a life sentence. To know how his status lay at the Yard and what it had done with his information of 30 October would be very useful in deciding what defence to run.

Lundy argued that Winship was twisting his motives. All he had done was calm down a distressed Mrs Garner in a telephone call, which he reported as soon as he arrived at work. Winship moved up a gear; Lundy's motives were capable of other interpretations. He reminded him that the *World In Action* programme 'The Untouchable' had alleged that his relationship with Garner was at best unprofessional and at worst corrupt. In Winship's view, what Lundy had done could form the basis of a charge to pervert the course of justice. What was more, the information he had passed on could also form the basis of a charge under the Official Secrets Act.

The meeting concluded with Winship telling Lundy that he was formally cautioning him, as he was required to do under the Police and Criminal Evidence Act, and that consequently Lundy was not required to say anything more. Within days Tony Lundy was suspended from duty.

Chrastny's confessions were a major breakthrough for the

Customs investigators. In time, they hoped to arrest everybody he had named. The immediate problem was keeping their star witness alive. They were under no illusions about how many people, in very different walks of life, might want him dead. It seemed too risky to leave him in one of London's prisons.

They came up with an extraordinary plan. The same day that Garner was charged, Chrastny was given bail, but he was not released. It was a legal device; the small print on his bail conditions said that he had to reside wherever the Customs officers wanted. He was taken straight from court, driven up the M1 to Yorkshire and lodged in the police station at Rotherham. There he would be safe from assassins and, just as importantly, he would be in the hands of the South Yorkshire police who were investigating the allegations in the *World In Action* programme about Garner and Lundy.

Chrastny was interviewed at length by the South Yorkshire detectives but his stay ended abruptly after 19 days. A perceptive Chief Superintendent noticed how Chrastny was 'ingratiating' himself with his officers. He had to be moved, before he could escape. The Customs officers and the South Yorkshire detectives cast around for a safer place to hold him. A few miles further north up the M1 in the West Yorkshire police area, midway between Leeds and Huddersfield, was Dewsbury. The local police station had a secure holding area that had been used to house informants and the infamous Yorkshire Ripper. Chrastny would not escape from Dewsbury.

The West Yorkshire police began with the best of intentions. They drew up a set of orders code-named 'Operation December' which set out the conditions of his stay. He was there to protect his life; he would be held securely; his presence must remain secret and he should be available to Customs officers for their continuing interrogations. They put him in a special cell which opened into a small hallway with a barred gate. The area was searched and he was locked up. From then on, the guarding of Chrastny went rapidly downhill.

He manipulated the police brilliantly. Chrastny exploited his captors' desire to keep him in a co-operative frame of mind. Everyone at Dewsbury found him 'affable and exceptionally polite'. The Rotherham warning was forgotten. He persuaded the officers to allow him a TV and a stereo. As there was no socket in his cell, the door had to be left open to allow a power lead to be run in from the doctor's room across the corridor.

Soon he played his TV and stereo late and loud into the night. He complained that he could not sleep because of the drunks in adjoining cells and so was not woken until mid-morning. The periods he remained unsupervised lengthened and nobody thought to ask how he was occupying his time. His wife Charlotte visited weekly and the guards were baffled by their conversations in German. Inexplicably she was permitted to give him £500 in cash. To while away his time he was allowed modelling plasticine, paint and glue.

In late September and again in early October, Chrastny was taken to London for identification parades. As he returned from the second trip a police officer noticed a suspicious black car outside the cell block. Then Chrastny was told that he would leave Dewsbury on 6 October.

In the early hours of 5 October, Chrastny finished sawing through the bars of his outer cell gate. He had been at it for several nights, removing his saw blades from their hiding place in the spine of a hardback book and disguising the incisions with the plasticine and paint. He then went into the doctor's room, open because of the extension lead used to power his television, through the window, out into the yard and away. In all probability the suspicious black car was waiting for him, with his old ally Lee Bryan at the wheel.

The next morning his jailers found a note on his bed, thanking them for their many kindnesses. Later in the day, at the Customs offices in New Fetter Lane, an officer heard the ringing tone from a vodaphone they had confiscated when Chrastny was captured. He answered, and to his surprise it was Chrastny on the other end. Chrastny, who thought the phone was still in his wife's possession, was equally amazed. He collected himself, thanked Customs and Excise for their hospitality, and rang off.

Chrastny's escape was good news for everybody named in his confession, but the cocaine trial would not start for another 18 months and in the interim both Garner and Lundy had more immediate problems. The South Yorkshire detectives had arrived in London and immediately discovered a curious set of events at the Old Bailey. A year earlier a young criminal, Lennie Leathers, had admitted a series of armed robberies in

7 The catamaran *Katlyn*, used to bring drugs upriver in Cornwall

8 The smuggling ship *Aquilon*, which brought drugs from Panama

9 Rubber fuel tanks in which drugs were concealed on the *Aquilon*

10 The Laurels, Tony Lundy's former home

11 65 Harley Street

12 Van der Breen, the drug guardian

13 Packaged cocaine retrieved in the Harley Street raid

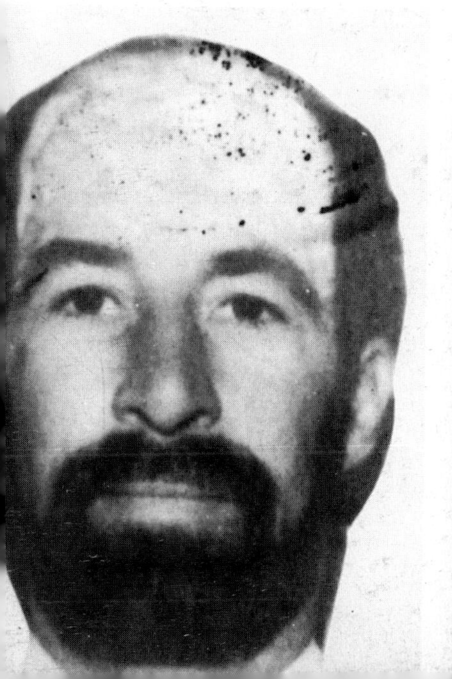

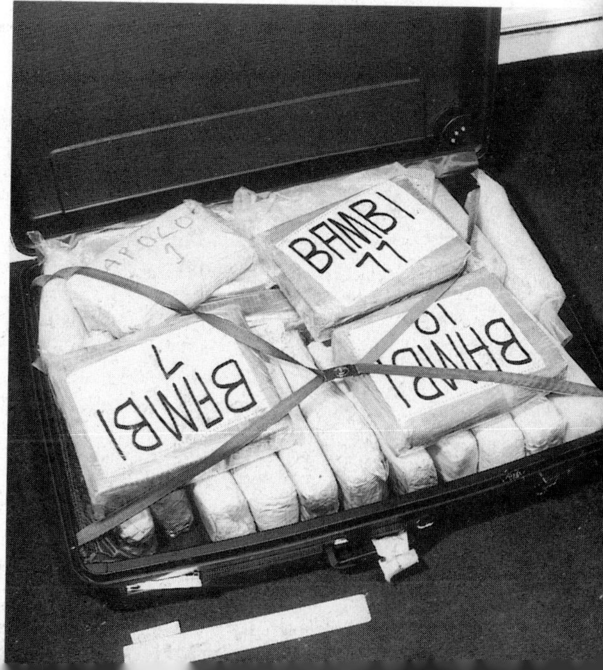

14 Tony Lundy, retired in Spain

15 Tony Lundy finishes the London Marathon, 1988

North London. As a detective was about to charge him, Lundy arrived in his office. 'Don't charge him,' said Lundy, 'the man is my grass.' Leathers was charged, but Lundy's attempts to help him did not stop there.

What happened next was summed up by the Complaints Authority in characteristically opaque language. There was an allegation that 'Lundy interfered in the sentencing of a criminal at the Old Bailey in early November 1986, a case with which Mr Lundy was not directly involved, on the basis that the criminal concerned had assisted the Met Police with their inquiries, a basis with which a number of Met Police colleagues would not agree.'

Behind this accusation lay a curious story. Lennie Leathers was a well-connected criminal. His wife's uncle was Les Jones, the millionaire scrap dealer and demolition contractor, who had holidayed with Lundy in Las Vegas in February 1980. By now Les Jones had bought Holborn Stud Farm, Garner's former country seat.

Leathers came up for sentence at the Old Bailey on 13 October 1986, three weeks before the screening of 'The Untouchable'. Lundy was seen outside the court talking to counsel. Leathers admitted three robbery charges but was remanded for sentence because two other men were pleading not guilty. The case lasted a month, by which time Lundy was away in America.

On Friday 7 November, four days after the screening of 'The Untouchable' Lundy was replaced at the Old Bailey by Detective Chief Superintendent Roy Ramm. He too had private discussions with counsel. The court did not sit until the afternoon. The Judge, having been briefed that Leathers was a valued informant and deserved a reduced penalty, jailed him for five years, half of what he might have expected. He smiled and said, 'Thank you.'

The secret row over whether Leathers was an informant who deserved a lenient sentence or whether justice had been perverted that day at the Old Bailey would simmer until the end of Lundy's police career. If Leathers was not an informant then Lundy, the detective who made his name publicly jailing armed robbers, had secretly put one criminal back on the street sooner than he deserved.

The Yorkshire detectives also looked at the allegation that Lundy had taken a quantity of wooden fencing from Stevie Salter in the mid-1970s. Salter had refused to talk to the Stagg inquiry. But by 1987 Salter's fortunes had changed. He had been jailed for three years for a fraud and the Yorkshire detectives visited him in prison. Salter wavered. Near the end of his sentence he was allowed out on home leave and promptly decamped to Belgium. Lengthy negotiations followed and Salter agreed to return and make a statement in which he revealed the name of the driver who helped him deliver the timber.

When the detectives traced that driver, now living in North Hertfordshire, he had a splendid memory not only of the layout of Lundy's former house in Cowley Hill Road, but also of the terms of the deal. There was only one load of timber and it was all delivered to Lundy. He did not see either an invoice or money handed over.

Lundy was in difficulties. When Stagg had challenged him years previously about the fencing allegation he had denied the story outright. Now he had two witnesses against him. Lundy's answer was to remember that, yes, he had after all received some timber, but not from Salter. It had been purchased by his good friend the former bookmaker David Spicer, who had sold some to him. Spicer even made a statement to back up this story. South Yorkshire was unimpressed by Spicer's recollections and deemed his statement 'non-relevant'.

The final and most serious accusation was the easiest to deal with. Lundy had been suspended immediately after his early morning phone conversation with Garner's wife. The Yorkshire detectives did not take long to make up their minds about that one.

The investigators went home to Yorkshire just before Christmas 1987. They had no doubt that the result of their inquiries should be corruption charges. They submitted a number of reports; some went to the Met and the Complaints Authority, others to the Director of Public Prosecutions.

The result was revealed by the Authority on 1 August 1988. Lundy had been suspended for 13 months and a decision on what to do with him was overdue. He was not to be charged with any crimes but he would face three disciplinary charges at a Tribunal. If found guilty, Lundy could be sacked. But neither the Authority nor Yard has ever publicly revealed what the charges were about.

The most serious charge was headed: 'Internal Enquiry into Leak to Confidential Informant.' It stated that Lundy had 'communicated to Mrs Roy Garner information which you had as a member of a police force: in that you told her that she could tell her husband that certain information had been passed at a very senior level from Scotland Yard to senior personnel of the agency dealing with his case.' The charge lent credibility to the allegation Chrastny had made to his Customs and Excise interrogators: that Lundy could help Garner. Now, in August 1988, Lundy stood accused of exactly that: passing on confidential information about the investigation into the cocaine conspiracy to help Roy Garner.

The Lennie Leathers affair resulted in another charge; Lundy was accused of misleading senior officers into telling the judge at Leathers's trial that the man in the dock was a helpful police informant. The fencing allegedly provided by Salter made up the third and final charge. There was a strong discipline case on two counts; Lundy had misled the Stagg inquiry and had taken a gift from Salter. It should have been enough to get him sacked.

Lundy's supporters hailed the decision not to prosecute him as a vindication of their man. The magazine *Police Review*, whose source for their story was Lundy himself, confidently revealed that 'the substance of the charges against Mr Lundy amount to no more than a failure to comply with an internal memorandum'.

Had Lundy faced criminal charges he would have been compelled to attend court and be judged. But for all its imposing title, the Disciplinary Tribunal was no threat; it could be shrugged off easily. From the moment Lundy's Tribunal was announced on 1 August everybody on the inside track, detectives, journalists and lawyers, knew it was unlikely ever to take place. Disciplinary Tribunals had been evaded by scores of detectives in the past.

Immediately after his interview with DAC Winship, Lundy succumbed to a mystery illness. It manifested itself in novel ways. He was fit enough to prepare himself for interview by the Yorkshire detectives and he kept up his daily ten-mile runs around the Hertfordshire countryside. In April 1988 he completed the London Marathon.

Now it was time to celebrate the failure of the Yorkshire investigation. Two weeks after the announcement that he would not face corruption charges Lundy submitted a planning application to his local council. He wanted to construct a swimming pool complex in the grounds of The Laurels. It would be a single-storey, 30 × 50 foot building with brickwork to match the house. Inside was a swimming pool, changing rooms, gym area, a sauna and a bar. The estimated cost was £250,000. Lundy was already planning to have a lot of time on his hands.

Garner had a brief outing from his remand cell to the Old Bailey in September 1988. He was charged with corrupting a prison warder while serving his sentence for the gold fraud in Ford open prison. Also charged were his son Mark and his wife June. A prison officer, Kenneth Colquhoun, had eased the burden of his incarceration by smuggling in some 'little luxuries'. These included jellied eels, bottles of vodka, roast chicken, smoked salmon, champagne, cigars and a little fresh fruit. Colquhoun was paid £3,000 for his services.

All three pleaded guilty. The Judge told them that the public might find it hard to understand how a man in prison could be dining on champagne and smoked salmon. In such circumstances, he said, 'the whole concept of punishment is undermined'. He gave Roy Garner 18 months and Mark 12 months. In a rare display of family fondness, both husband and son kissed June on the cheek before being taken down to start their sentences.

The court then dealt with June Garner. Her barrister, June Southworth, made a stirring mitigation plea. Although her client's social report described her as 'resilient', June Garner had been under a lot of strain recently. This strain was particularly acute following a TV programme in which 'wild statements' were made that Roy Garner was an informant.

In the dock June Garner started to cry. Judge Scrivener said that although wives who smuggle goods into their husbands 'must expect to go to jail', he could not bring himself to give her a custodial sentence, 'seeing you there suffering'. He gave her 12 months, suspended for two years.

A second TV film about Lundy and Garner was in preparation. This programme, again from *World In Action*, would deal with the drugs conspiracy. The journalists knew that Lundy had been named by Chrastny. They had also learned the devastating nature of the discipline charges. Now they discovered that Lundy was planning to leave the Yard without facing his Disciplinary Tribunal. The first date for his Tribunal came and went. He was too ill to attend. A story was published in *Private Eye* predicting that Lundy was on his way out. It was up to Commissioner Imbert to decide whether Lundy could go, or would be forced to attend the hearing. On 22 December Scotland Yard released the following statement.

'After a protracted illness Detective Superintendent Tony Lundy has been declared permanently unfit for police work and will therefore retire from the Metropolitan Police on Friday December 23, 1988. This follows an examination by the Chief Medical Officer of the Metropolitan Police and a second, independent, medical opinion. The Home Office has been advised. Detective Superintendent Lundy was suspended from duty in 1987.'

How many minds agonised over the wording and timing of this shamefully inadequate statement can only be imagined. It was released by the sophisticated Scotland Yard press office just prior to the Christmas holiday, when the news media is not at its sharpest. Letting Lundy retire on an index-linked medical pension meant that both the detective and the Yard would be spared the embarrassment of a Disciplinary Tribunal.

The Complaints Authority which had overseen the two-year investigation by South Yorkshire was furious. It released its own statement. Judged by the standards of the usual 'Yes, Minister' language employed by civil servants, it screamed indignation.

> The Police Complaints Authority have now been informed by Scotland Yard that the Metropolitan Police have granted Detective Superintendent Lundy medical retirement which means that he will not appear before a Disciplinary Tribunal. The Authority have no role in the decision to grant medical retirement and they regret that there will now be no opportunity either to prove or disprove the charges at a disciplinary hearing.

Despite the Authority's indignation the Yard had achieved what many sceptics believed to be its objectives. There would be no messy Disciplinary Tribunal, and when the cocaine trial started in the New Year, whatever embarrassment might be caused by allegations about Lundy, they would no longer be allegations about a serving police officer.

The *World In Action* journalists had, unknown to Lundy, filmed him completing the London Marathon six months earlier, while he was officially sick. They were also aware that, despite his alleged ill-health, he was still running every day. Seven days before the Scotland Yard announcement that Lundy was retiring on health grounds, *World In Action* happened upon Lundy running near his home in Hertfordshire. They attempted to ask him about his involvement with Garner and allegations that he was corrupt. Lundy refused to speak and, despite his 'protracted illness', eventually outran the camera crew.

20 · ON TRIAL

THE TRIAL OF ROY GARNER ought, by rights, to have been held in Court One at the Old Bailey. The enormity of the crime, conspiring to import and distribute £100 million worth of cocaine, deserved nothing less. But the historic Court One, always the venue for the biggest trials, was not available. Its intimacy, so appropriate for the showdown, was already booked for a spy trial. The cases had similar cores; both men were accused of seeking to undermine British society. Both trials would also hear evidence in secret.

So when Garner came up the steps from the cells on 23 January 1989, he found himself in the dock of Court Two. Waiting was his counsel, the flamboyant and portly Michael Corkery, and Customs' mild-mannered prosecutor, Derek Spencer. From the press benches it looked like the Public School Establishment Man versus the Bright Grammar School Boy. Above them all, on the bench, sat the forbidding and skeletal figure of Judge Kenneth Machin. Alongside Garner in the dock was Charlotte Chrastny and two minor criminals, associates of the missing Micky Henessey. That line-up, without Chrastny or Henessey, was to be described in the course of the trial as Hamlet without the Prince, Rosencrantz or Guildenstern. Some thought that one more member of the cast list was missing.

In the months before the case came to the Old Bailey the

Customs men were spreading the word that their best odds were 50–50. Chrastny was always going to be their key witness, and without the lengthy statement he had made just before his escape from Dewsbury, their case against Roy Garner was weakened.

With Chrastny gone, Garner's defence would be one of disbelief at his predicament; the innocent man who knew nothing about cocaine. However, there was a problem. When Garner had taken his day off from jail in October 1986 to go to Scotland Yard to try to stop the *World in Action* programme he had disclosed both his inside knowledge of the crime and of the police investigation into it. That meeting had been taped. His counsel, Michael Corkery, had to prevent the transcript of that meeting being entered as evidence.

If Corkery failed, then the alternative defence was to admit that Garner was involved, but only so he could inform on the crime. But once the defence went down that road, they would have to go the whole way. All Garner's long-documented record of informing for the Yard would have to be brought out in front of the jury. Inevitably, Garner's long-time handler at the Yard, Tony Lundy, would have to be called to back him up.

A few days into the New Year the word was out among the Old Bailey reporters; they had picked up the intelligence that Lundy, who would inevitably and impressively claim to be one of the Yard's greatest ever detectives, was on standby to speak up for Garner.

Now Spencer, the prosecution counsel, had to gamble. If Lundy appeared he could swing the trial either way; if he looked credible and honest the jury might believe that Garner was honest. But if the relationship between Lundy and Garner looked dubious, Spencer was heading for a victory. So the famous crime-buster would have to be discredited before he could show his face at the Bailey. In the classic sporting metaphor, Spencer would have to get his retaliation in first. He did.

The prosecution case could have been built on little more than the fact that cocaine had been found in London and witnesses could place Garner with Chrastny in Florida. Spencer decided to go further. He would argue that part of the contract Garner offered Chrastny was a guarantee of protection direct from Scotland Yard. There were two sources of proof; witnesses would testify to this 'clause' and, in the event, the cocaine gang *had* been tipped off that an investigation was underway.

Spencer's warning shot must have sent a shiver down the spines of Lundy, Garner and the defence team. A couple of hours into his opening speech the prosecution counsel gave the first hint of his tactics when he mentioned, for no apparent reason, that Garner had been visited in jail by a man called Lundy who was a Scotland Yard detective. The aside was lost amidst the fascinating chronology of the cocaine trafficking and was hardly reported the next day.

If Spencer appeared low-key, his tactics were not. The prosecution's ace card was Roy Whitehorne, who had been granted immunity in return for giving Queen's Evidence. He was always going to describe the crucial meeting between Garner and Chrastny in Fort Lauderdale in the spring of 1984 to set up the deal. Now more was required. He did not falter.

The first bombshell landed on 30 January and it was Black Monday for Lundy. Whitehorne was talking about visiting Garner's luxury apartment at Pompano Beach. He recalled, 'On one occasion I was kept waiting. I was told that there were police in the apartment "from here". Later I was told a name. Lundy was one of them. Lundy was working at Scotland Yard . . . I was led to believe that he was a very high-ranking officer.'

Spencer led his witness further into the plot. 'Was anything said about safety?' Whitehorne obliged. 'Roy was trying to assure Charles that it would be safe because of the contacts he had at Scotland Yard. Two people were mentioned by name. The third I remembered because I met him once. It was Lundy . . . He said he would be notified if there was any kind of trouble.'

The presses rolled and the next day's papers carried Whitehorne's clear implication that Lundy was a member of the plot, the co-conspirator, the gang's inside man at the Yard. Lundy, who a decade earlier had revelled in feeding the press the lines they loved about the Great War Against Crime, was impotent. He would be forced into the witness box as much to record his denials as to back Garner.

Spencer had more damaging evidence to lead. He invited Whitehorne to talk about his visits to Britain during the conspiracy. 'I had a dinner engagement with Roy Garner, his wife and friends at a restaurant . . . someone was talking to Roy Garner, I'd no idea who it was. I was told, "Its Old Bill." Lundy was leaving and we did not speak to each other.' Spencer inquired, mildly, 'How did you find out that the "Old Bill" was Lundy?' Whitehorne replied, 'Later I was told that's who it was.'

Again the presses rolled and there for all to see was Lundy dragged deeper into the cocaine conspiracy. But Spencer had yet another card to play. He moved on to the next revelation, that the gang were tipped off about the secret surveillance being mounted by Minto and Breece through Tullevere.

He led Whitehorne through the frenetic phone calls between members of the gang at the end of the first week of October 1986; calls to Fort Lauderdale from both London and Los Angeles. 'I was informed by everyone that my telephone had a tap . . . Charles, a friend of Garner and Mark Garner all told me.'

Spencer: 'How did they know?'

Whitehorne: 'They'd been informed by people at Scotland Yard . . . They were all calling at the same time. They'd all got the message at the same time for me to keep off my telephone.'

Whitehorne did not have it his own way all the time. When Spencer sat down, Corkery harried and blasted Whitehorne for more than a week over his dubious past and alleged lies. Braving the increasing yawns of Judge Machin and perhaps ignoring the same behaviour in the jury ranks Corkery played many of the Tullevere tapes, inevitably picking on ones that he interpreted as Whitehorne being party to various criminal conspiracies, which, of course, the witness denied. Corkery declared later that Garner's solicitor, crouched over his notebook in the well of the court, had recorded no fewer than 146 accusations of lying.

But this fine display of energy could not prevent more disasters for Lundy, who was fast becoming Corkery's unofficial second client. Spencer now produced the two Americans who had worked for Chrastny. They were pleading guilty and had agreed to give evidence for the Crown. On 8 February came Brian Van der Breen, who had helped import the drugs. He remembered that 'Charles said that people he had been dealing with were told to leave town by Scotland Yard'. During cross-examination later Van der Breen said that Chrastny told him he 'owned someone at Scotland Yard'. The other American, Robert Cermack, who had been the cocaine baby-sitter at Harley Street, told a similar story. 'Charles had a contact at Scotland Yard. If anything were to start going wrong, he would be told through his contact.'

For another two weeks more witnesses trooped through Court Two, but always at the back of Corkery's mind was the problem of the Scotland Yard tape. He had hoped to make it, and Garner's damaging disclosures, inadmissible but Spencer had outmanoeuvred him. The prosecution, having been forced to declare open season on Lundy, was firing every available round. Buried in the tape were Garner's confirmation of his relationship with Lundy, denials that the detective was crooked and also the damaging disclosure that Garner knew the cocaine conspiracy was under investigation.

Corkery's only possible ploy was to make a virtue of Garner's record, true or not, of being the Yard's biggest ever informant. But both Garner and Lundy would want such evidence to be divulged behind closed doors. Garner, naturally, feared retribution. Lundy needed secrecy because he knew the circumstances of his leaving the Yard and the nature of the discipline charges he had avoided were bound to be raised.

On the afternoon of Wednesday 22 February Corkery won Judge Machin's consent for the court to go into chambers for what was described 'as an administrative matter'. We can never know what was said in that hearing, and if we did, we could not report it. But there was only one direction in which the now secret trial could proceed. Corkery was bound to argue that Spencer's tactics had forced him to drop Garner's 'I am totally innocent' pose and substitute the 'I had knowledge of the conspiracy but only so I could inform on these evil men' ploy. For safety reasons, such evidence would have to be taken *in camera* with press and public excluded.

Spencer would have been certain to respond with the newly established 'Spycatcher' principle that the information about Garner was already in the public domain, through the *World In Action* programme of November 1986 and subsequent press coverage. He may have added that the informant system is based on the belief that the detective who handles the informant is honest and that the informant is genuine and not a participant in the crime. Seeing that Spencer had deliberately called Lundy's integrity into question earlier in open court he was bound to argue in private that Lundy was a dishonest detective and so the public interest required public disclosure.

Journalists waiting outside the court were intrigued to see Detective Chief Inspector John Grieve called as a witness. It is not a state secret that Grieve had been staff officer to DAC Brian Worth. Grieve was involved in running the informants system and also part of the team of officers who had successfully blocked the BBC *Brass Tacks* programme about Lundy and Garner. Again, we cannot know what he told the court but it must be the case that he argued for Garner's role as an informant to be kept confidential.

Eventually the press and public were allowed back into court and Judge Machin gave his ruling on the secret arguments he had just heard. After stating the fundamental principle that justice should be in public, Machin explained why he was going to abandon it. Apparently Corkery had submitted that if the court did not sit *in camera* he would not be able to adduce 'certain matters'. Once more, the press and public trooped out of court.

Machin's ruling was undoubtedly made in good faith, but the *in camera* proceedings were at first a farce and eventually an affront to justice. They undoubtedly protected the dubious Garner/Lundy relationship from long-overdue public scrutiny. At worst, the court may have been misled about the extent of Lundy's knowledge of the cocaine conspiracy, his alleged involvement in the tip-off to the gang and the truth about the discipline charges he escaped. Of course we can never know the exact words spoken in Court Two after the wooden shutters went up on the windows in the double doors — but we can guess.

The first *in camera* witness was DCS Roy Ramm. The essential piece of evidence that Spencer wanted Ramm to produce was the transcript of the October 1986 meeting. We know this because at Garner's committal at Guildhall magistrates in the spring of 1988 Ramm had done exactly that and nobody had thought to go *in camera*.

Ramm's evidence at the Guildhall shocked and angered the Customs' Redskin team. They had had no idea that Garner had told so much about the cocaine smuggling to Worth and Ramm at the very time when he was a prime target for the crime. They were equally unaware that the Yard had taped the meeting. For 18 months the Yard failed to reveal to the Customs officers the information Garner had volunteered about Britain's biggest ever cocaine importation. Customs believe that if they had been told at the time they might well have seized much more of the 392 kilos before it hit the streets.

So the first part of Ramm's secret evidence can be accurately assessed. Spencer would have picked on the sections of the conversation implicating Garner in the cocaine conspiracy. Unfortunately we will never know if he referred Ramm to his comment, on tape, about Garner 'pissing himself with laughter' at that secret meeting.

It is highly likely that Ramm, in cross-examination by Corkery, vouched for Lundy's probity and for his record as a detective. He would also have confirmed that Lundy was Garner's handler and former Commander Corbett the controller. Indeed Corbett came from his new post as a security officer at the Bank of England and waited outside Court Two to give evidence for Garner but was never called.

It is also likely that Ramm repeated what he said at the Guildhall: that Garner wanted the *World in Action* film stopped and that the criminal was never cautioned because Ramm and his boss, DAC Worth, head of Specialist Operations, had absolutely no idea that Garner was already the subject of a specialist Yard drugs operation, code-named Operation Distant Drum.

After Ramm's answers to Corkery, prosecution counsel Spencer would have needed to re-examine his witness. Spencer was declaring Lundy to be corrupt so Ramm would probably have been asked about the disciplinary charges dodged by Lundy. By far the most important charge was Lundy's leak about the cocaine investigation to Mrs Garner, at her husband's request.

Ramm would have had the choice of playing down the affair as some kind of unauthorised disclosure that happened to involve Mrs Garner — or making the blunt point the jury was entitled to hear: that Lundy was accused of a serious leak of information about the cocaine investigation, was given a criminal caution, and then suspended a few days later. It is unimaginable that an officer of Ramm's rank would have done other than tell the jury the full truth.

Ramm's evidence was punctuated on Friday 4 February by a brave incursion from the *Observer* newspaper which sought to have the *in camera* farce stopped. Initially Judge Machin slapped a contempt order on the speech from their barrister, Heather Rogers, but later in the day he generously agreed to permit publication. The jury was of course sent out during Rogers's comments but could read them two days later in the *Observer*. Suddenly the subtext of the trial was dramatically revealed. 'Allegations of corrupt links between a senior Metropolitan police detective and a man on trial on £100 million cocaine smuggling charges were publicly disclosed on Friday at the Old Bailey . . . ' ran the report.

> 'The defendant, London businessman Roy Garner, had been identified as having a role as a police informer and had been accused of having a corrupt relationship with Detective Superintendent Tony Lundy,' Ms Heather Rogers, counsel for the *Observer*, told the court. 'Mr Lundy had been investigated over his relationship with Garner in two police inquiries,' she said. 'There are very grave concerns on the part of the public and the press . . . public-concern has continued since Mr Lundy retired from the police while facing disciplinary charges, it is said on health grounds.'

The story may have been the turning point in the trial. The next day Garner was seen to have a temporary fainting fit and stumble as he left the dock at lunchtime. On the following Friday the Garner case received another jolt. It was a warm afternoon and in the absence of the jury Corkery was submitting that Whitehorne's evidence had been dangerous and should be struck out. For 20 minutes Corkery went *in camera*, and when the court re-opened one of the authors was the only journalist in the court.

The barrister was bemoaning his problems; what hope could he have when the jury knew that his client was a major criminal? Seeming to forget that the court was again in open session Corkery pointed out that the jury now knew Garner was an informant as well. The jealously guarded days *in camera* were suddenly blown and his junior, Oliver Sells, seeing the journalist's pen suddenly scurrying across the page, rolled his eyes upwards. But Corkery was oblivious to danger and, minutes later, reinforced his point, adding that the jury now knew that Garner was 'an informant and bounty hunter'.

Suddenly Corkery realised his mistake. Shamefacedly he announced, 'I hope the press will behave honourably.' Judge Machin was less sure and, retrospectively, imposed a contempt order on Corkery's slips of the tongue. It was lifted at the end of the trial.

The trial continued into the second week of March and Lundy was spotted in the Old Bailey tearoom. With him was Commander Ray Adams, who had yet to be cleared of corruption allegations. Ramm was there as well and the three spoke quietly. The press were back in hordes as word spread that Lundy was about to give evidence for Garner.

At 10.03 Corkery called the suntanned Lundy and took him through his commendations. Lundy's harsh Lancastrian accent lacked grace as he made the very best of the good points of his career. He denied all the earlier allegations in the trial. After 30 minutes Corkery applied to go *in camera* and Spencer was on his feet, not to object but to insist that Detective Inspector Dave Wilson, from the South Yorkshire Police, who had sat through every day of the trial, be allowed to stay. Corkery objected but Machin allowed Wilson to go on taking his meticulous notes.

For everyone else, the doors closed again, the shutters went up and the public was denied the right to see Lundy tested on oath. It was another defeat for justice and, as was revealed later, a chance for Lundy to tell his own, unchallenged, version of the story of Special Agent Mike Breece and the package of tapes in secret. But whatever Lundy said on Garner's behalf was not enough. On Wednesday 22 March 1989 justice caught up with Garner when the jury pronounced him guilty; on the Thursday, Judge Machin called him an evil man and sent him away for 22 years and on the next day, Good Friday, the world was a slightly better place to live in. The peace was disturbed only by Lundy's bizarre insistence that Garner was innocent and that the prosecution had been a vendetta by Customs. For no obvious reason Lundy also volunteered the news that he was a practising Catholic.

For the journalists at *World in Action*, their second film would be the product of five years' research and nine months of concentrated work, travel and secret meetings with sources. The programme was given an uncompromising title, 'Scotland Yard's Cocaine Connection', but it would not be screened for another ten days. Meanwhile, the discredited Lundy was signed up for £20,000 by the *News of the World* for a two-part series. Despite the cautious headline 'Bent Or Brilliant' the tabloid seemed to plump for the latter view. Lundy rejected the results of the South Yorkshire inquiry as 'trumped-up' and a 'frame'. He also made outrageous claims about his successes; one being the use of supergrass David Smith. None of the *News of the World* reporters seemed aware of Smith's grisly suicide in a police cell. At the end of the article readers were invited to phone in with their personal views; was Lundy a saint or a sinner?

The following week's issue did not reveal the poll result. Instead there was a picture of an awkward-looking Lundy in collar, tie and blazer on holiday in the Spanish sun. He blamed his problems on the Freemasons and claimed that it was he who had spent years investigating Roy Garner! By now the *News of the World* must have been thoroughly confused about why it had given Lundy £20,000. The best line in the whole page was a generous plug for the next day's *World In Action* programme which clearly had obtained much more exciting material for a lot less money.

On the Monday night 'Scotland Yard's Cocaine Connection' produced the Tullevere tapes that Corkery had not used, in which Whitehorne boasted about their man at the Yard. It also disclosed the contents of Chrastny's statement. The sequence of Lundy on his daily run, filmed a few days before the Yard declared him permanently disabled, was also featured. Florida Special Agent Mike Breece was seen talking about the package of tapes and his conversations with Lundy which had accidently revealed the existence of the undercover cocaine investigation into Garner.

In the month following the trial it became clear that a transcript of what had been said behind closed doors at the Old Bailey had been liberated. On 12 April 1989 the editor of the *Observer* wrote to the Attorney General giving notice of his intention to publish some of the forbidden material. The paper claimed that evidence given *in camera* 'was misleading and inaccurate . . . furthermore, we know that HM Customs accused Lundy of corruption and leaking information to a criminal.' The letter revealed that a transcript of the *in camera* evidence was circulating in the United States and that *Observer* reporters had had a chance to study it.

The *Observer* did publish, on 23 April 1989. The story said:

> Lawyers representing HM Customs accused a senior Scotland Yard detective of corruption in a secret session during an Old Bailey drugs trial . . . Lundy was cross-examined *in camera* about two leaks to the cocaine smugglers which occurred after he allegedly gained knowledge of the case. His answers were inconsistent with subsequent statements by Florida police.
>
> Mr Derek Spencer, cross-examing him for Customs, said the nature of the corrupt relationship was that Garner gave Lundy information to further his career and Lundy gave Garner police information. He told Lundy: 'You found out Garner was being inquired into and you told him.' Lundy denied the allegations.

The *Observer* then turned to the package of tapes Agent Breece so nearly entrusted to Lundy in Florida. Apparently Lundy had told the Old Bailey jury, 'I do not know . . . I never knew the contents of the package.' However, on the *World in Action* film the Florida police officer who handled the package was asked: 'Mr Lundy now knew that tapes were going from Fort Lauderdale to Sgt Gordon Bain at Scotland Yard?' Special Agent Michael Breece replied: 'Yes, he did.' Neither the Attorney General or Judge Machin has seen it proper to take action against the *Observer* for these disclosures.

Meanwhile the flow of corruption allegations continued. Chrastny's wife Charlotte had been found guilty of conspiring to import and distribute the cocaine and was soon back at the Old Bailey to face the charge of aiding and abetting her husband's escape from Dewsbury police station. She was acquitted but then jailed for seven years for her cocaine conviction and ordered to forfeit more than £2.6 million seized by the Customs' Redskin team.

The court heard that the Dewsbury police had drawn up Operation December, a set of dramatically titled rules for Chrastny's stay. The reason, they stated, was to protect his life and prevent his escape. The first witness for the prosecution was Customs man Bob Gray, the Redskin case officer. He was cross-examined by Mrs Chrastny's counsel, Timothy Cassels.

Cassels: Chrastny had also given evidence about corruption in the police: who was involved?

Grey: Lundy and Garner.

Cassels: A number of people would have an interest in Chrastny's escape?

Grey: Yes.

Cassels: New Scotland Yard, for instance?

Grey: I cannot comment on that.

In past years Cassels had prosecuted many of Lundy's cases, most memorably representing the Crown at the sentencing of Gibson and the other Silver Bullion robbers. Now, in his summing up, he did not mince his words. Cassels spelled out what the media, the detectives and the criminal world were all saying privately. 'A number of people had a motive for helping Chrastny escape,' asserted Cassels to the jury. Top of his list was 'New Scotland Yard'.

21 · THE POWERS THAT BE

IN EARLY JANUARY 1989 two of the authors were sitting with Special Agent Mike Minto in an unmarked police car watching Chrastny's secluded house in Broward County, Florida. We asked Minto, what had been his view of Scotland Yard in the past? 'Motherhood and apple pie,' he said, and we laughed. He knew we would enjoy the cliché but there was a glint in his eyes that made the follow-up question inevitable. 'And your opinion now?' The smile disappeared. 'I hope your Parliament is going to be able to do something to clear all this up.'

We heard the same concerns from California and also from Wiesbaden. Similarly, in the pubs around New Fetter Lane the always deniable conversations turned to how far Scotland Yard could be trusted, and what ought to be done to reform the CID. Every law enforcement officer we met had a story of the good guys at the Yard — detectives like Sergeant Gordon Bain — who had shared information with Customs and Excise and eschewed glory in the fight against organised crime. But there was always the same refrain: corruption and incompetence are alive and well at the Yard. Worse still, when caught out, the reaction is, too often, one of cover-up and deceit.

During the years spent researching the saga of Garner and Lundy we came up against some of the worst features of the Yard; obstruction, lies, and improper surveillance. Much more depressing was their inability to recognise that anything wrong might have happened. These reactions came largely from the upper ranks. The nearer we got to street level the more we found officers with the honesty and the courage to disclose information that the public has a right to know. Unfortunately, those officers were in a minority. Many Yard detectives saw nothing wrong in accepting invitations to Lundy's farewell party at a Lancaster Gate hotel in January 1989 on the eve of Garner's trial.

Belatedly the scandals did come to the House of Commons. The remorseless flow of disclosures over the years had made it inevitable, but Special Agent Minto would be saddened to see how the Metropolitan Police and their political masters so casually deflected the long-overdue questions.

The fault is in the system. The select committees that initiate these kinds of inquiries have limited resources. On Capitol Hill a scandal of the size of the 'Untouchable Overlord of London Crime' and the sudden retirement of the 'permanently sick marathon runner' would have sired an investigation by a committee of Congressmen. They would have been backed up by teams of lawyers, researchers and experts on policing and organised crime. Independent reports would have been prepared and the hearings led by experienced counsel. All relevant witnesses would have been summoned and required, on oath, to give evidence in public. Light would have been shone into the murkier areas of criminal investigation and, at the very least, the public would have discovered what had been done in their name and with their taxes.

Such an inquiry cannot happen in Britain. Institutions like the Met, with the support of their Parliamentary allies, have erected permanent shutters to keep the sunlight out. The saga of Lundy-Garner did come before our legislature; but the hearings of the Home Affairs Committee in the summer of 1989 are a perfect example of how Britain's premier policing agency, and the politicians we trust to oversee it, escape accountability.

Committee Room 15 at the House of Commons is a large, airy Gothic room with windows overlooking the Thames and fleur-de-lys flock wallpaper. In the centre is a horseshoe-shaped table around which sit the 11 members of the Home Affairs Committee. Witnesses sit at its open mouth and Members take turns to put questions. The Committee's brief is to monitor all aspects of Home Office responsibilities, including the police.

In the wake of the screening of the *World In Action* 'Scotland Yard's Cocaine Connection', 18 MPs, including former Home Secretary Merlyn Rees, had signed an Early Day Motion. In the rather breathless prose that such one-sentence motions must use, it ranged across their concerns. It began with the cocaine leak from the Yard; mentioned the surveillance by the Met on Andrew Jennings; noted that an officer named as 'corrupt', Detective Superintendent Lundy, had retired early before the resolution of the South Yorkshire investigation, and finally called on the Select Committee to examine the general allegation of corruption at the Yard.

The motion was drafted by Labour MP Clive Soley. A week later the Committee Chairman, Sir John Wheeler, voiced his concern about the *World In Action* programme, revealing that he had raised the issue with the Chairman of the Police Complaints Authority. The subject surfaced a fortnight later in the Authority's annual report. The language was low-key but the thrust was deadly. The Authority complained about its lack of power to complete inquiries into officers above the rank of Chief Superintendent; a direct reference to how the Yard had sidestepped the investigation into who ordered the surveillance on Jennings's former home in Islington.

Then the report turned to medical retirements. The insult the Authority suffered over Lundy's medical retirement was deeply felt, not least because of press suggestions that, ultimately, the Authority was impotent. Lundy had done no more than opt for the lucrative exit that his equally dubious predecessors had taken when investigations came too close. But the disclosure of his considerable physical fitness made ridiculous the claim that an independent police complaints authority could impose its will on the Met. The Authority had 'been robbed' and they knew it.

The Chairman, Sir Cecil Clothier, wrote in best Whitehall mandarin language that the affair was 'unsatisfactory'. This was code for the scandalised feelings that members of the Authority expressed in private. The Annual Report probably received more press coverage than any of its three predecessors. The *Sun* headline summed it up best: 'Bent Coppers Get Off.'

The first witnesses to appear before the microphones in Committee Room 15, in the late afternoon of 22 May 1989, were Sir Cecil and his two deputies, former Labour minister Roland Moyle and Brigadier John Pownall. It was the first of four hearings to examine the working of the Complaints Authority. Soon Clothier was complaining about 'the unsatisfactory role we are given with respect to complaints against senior officers, where our task is simply to supervise the investigation and hand it back to the appropriate authority to take action upon it as they feel fit. They are the adjudicators, which ordinarily we would be.'

There had been an attempt the previous year to raise the senior officers anomaly in the Commons, highlighted as it had been in previous Authority reports. Labour MP Jeremy Corbyn had asked a polite question of the then Home Secretary Douglas Hurd and was put down as a 'loony lefty'.

Cynics might have expected Committee Chairman Sir John Wheeler, an urbane Tory MP, to guide the hearings around the unpleasant disclosures that the years of investigations had uncovered. Few realised that he was formerly an assistant prison governor who knew what he was talking about. Wheeler got to the point early: 'It is fair to mention the sense of outrage that I think MPs and others would feel if early retirement seemed linked with impending disciplinary charges.'

Clothier took the cue. 'How disappointed we are that there was no final resolution of a complaint alleging quite serious breaches of discipline . . . we have incurred great public expenditure on the investigation of an allegation which was serious and then at the end, when very close to a resolution, the matter was snatched away.'

It was the Tory MP Dame Janet Foulkes who cut through the mannered discussion. 'Would you agree . . . the situation which has just been discussed looks like a cover-up, a white-wash, an attempt to cover over something nasty?'

Clothier glided through the door she had opened. 'You are speaking of Mr Lundy — there is no point in pretending we do not know what we are talking about — it is not so much that justice is not being done, as that justice is not being reached.'

Just who might be blocking justice was immediately seized on by Labour MP and barrister Gerry Bermingham. 'The decision that he was permitted to retire — I think that is the nicest way of putting it — meant that someone in the Home Office, or the Police Force, consented to his decision or application to retire on medical grounds?' Clothier agreed: in the weeks to come the hunt would switch from seeking the truth about Lundy to trying to discover the truth about who had let him go.

Bermingham wanted to know more. On what grounds could Lundy possibly claim protracted disability? Was his illness mental or physical? Clothier answered, 'We never saw the medical report.' At the back of Committee Room 15 there was a great deal of note-taking going on. The Metropolitan Police Commissioner, Sir Peter Imbert, had sent two detectives to bring him advance notice of how the land would lie when his turn came to appear.

At the second session, in the first week of June, a memorandum from the Association of Chief Police Officers admitted 'it is a fact that increasingly officers accused of disciplinary offences are successfully satisfying a doctor either that their attendance before a discipline board will be seriously detrimental to their health or that they are not medically fit to appear before such a board.' ACPO did not explain why they had taken so long to discover a trend that everyone else had known about for decades. The public embarrassment of the TV footage of Lundy running was at last concentrating their attention.

There was also a memorandum from the Police Federation. Their thoughts on medical retirement ran to one sentence: 'In the opinion of the Police Federation any decisions on medical retirement should be made by the Chief Officer.' This breathtaking lack of interest forced a question from Labour MP Tony Worthington. 'Here we have a situation where there is widespread public concern about senior officers avoiding disciplinary charges by obtaining medical retirement. Your Federation seems not to care at all?' The answer from Mr John Thompson, secretary of the Federation's Discipline sub-committee was uninspired. 'I do not see how you can tighten up the regulations.'

Throughout Britain local police authorities have a say in the running of their police forces. They control budgets and several times a year the Chief Constable must attend their meetings. The people of London are denied this privilege. The Met, for all practical purposes, is unaccountable to the people who pay for it. There is no democratic channel for the ratepayers of London to ask questions or voice criticisms.

The police authority for London is the Home Secretary.

Occasionally, in Parliament, he and his junior ministers may answer questions, but embarrassing issues can be sidestepped. Day-to-day responsibilities for supervising Britain's biggest police force, its billion-pound-a-year budget and its 30,000 officers are handled by a few civil servants at the Home Office. In practice the Met runs itself.

The Commissioner, Sir Peter Imbert, appeared at the third Parliamentary session. In advance he sent an astonishing memorandum, which attempted to discourage the Members from asking specific questions about the Lundy affair. In his memo Imbert did concede 'it is recognised there is a measure of concern in some quarters in respect of this case, which received considerable publicity, some of which is speculative. Therefore this opportunity to allay some of this concern is welcome.' But, he went on, 'unfortunately, there are constraints upon us.'

Despite the concerns already voiced by MPs in Committee Room 15, Imbert quoted to them their own standing orders which do not allow them to investigate individual cases. He continued, 'Such considerations ought to apply to the details of the investigation conducted into the allegations made against Mr Lundy and accordingly the Commissioner feels unable to answer specific questions.' So that was that.

The Commissioner arrived at Committee Room 15 on 12 June. Labour MP Joe Ashton picked his moment and pointed out that the Complaints Authority had expressed its concern about their lack of power in supervising investigations into the senior ranks. Then, quoting freely from a memorandum submitted to the Committee by two of the authors, Ashton raised the issue of the surveillance on Jennings and the fact that the Met had declared his complaint 'unsubstantiated'.

Imbert replied that the complaint *was* unsubstantiated. But Ashton was too experienced to be fobbed off so easily. He persisted until Imbert admitted that *if* there had been surveillance, and he would not confirm or deny, it would not have been improper. Imbert claimed that the South Yorkshire investigators had backed him on this.

John Wheeler then led the hearing on to medical retirements, inevitably Lundy's name came up and Imbert admitted 'the suggestion was being made that there had been some sinister reason for allowing a particular officer to retire'. Clearly this could not be the case but what he did disclose was that in the previous three years six Met officers had left with medical pensions while awaiting disciplinary hearings and a further 38 officers during the course of investigations.

Encouraged, Joe Ashton tried another approach. 'Are you satisfied that the prima facie evidence of misconduct by a Metropolitan Police officer in a major drugs case prosecuted by HM Customs and Excise will not permanently damage the essential co-operation in the fight against drugs?' Imbert's response was revealing. Accepting the thrust of Ashton's query he replied, 'I am satisfied that it will not *permanently* damage relationships at all.' There would be no further concessions by the Yard.

After three sessions Special Agent Minto's hopes of justice from the British Parliament would have been disappointed. Commissioner Imbert had come and gone and the list of unanswered questions was as long as before. Now it was the turn of the Home Office. Their Mr Eric Soden was even more determined to avoid becoming embroiled in a scandal. Quite simply, the Home Office had no plans to change the medical retirement rules.

The MPs tried again; they still wanted to know who had taken the decision to let Lundy go. Tony Worthington pressed, 'It is difficult to imagine a case which is more sensitive and more important, so would it be right to infer that the Home Secretary himself would have had an input into the Lundy case?' Soden blocked. 'It would be inappropriate for me to comment on an individual case.' It was not a good day for open government.

Frustrated, the MPs tried to widen the issues. Tony Worthington came forward again. 'Mr Lundy and some of his colleagues were investigated by Mr Steventon . . . there was a Detective Sergeant Miller . . . who was also retired with an enhanced medical pension, who was facing four disciplinary charges. You will be aware of that?'

Mr Soden was not aware. Worthington pressed on. 'But there was very great concern about a section of the Metropolitan Police, linked with Lundy, and here we have Mr Lundy, who retires on an enhanced medical pension, and in 1984 another member of the same group of people, who was facing four disciplinary charges, was retired on an enhanced medical pension without facing those charges, and you are saying to us there are no grounds for concern?' This of course Soden denied. He concluded with the breathtaking comment, 'I fail to see where the criticism lies.'

There was only one major revelation at the Select Committee hearings and it took an ambush to flush it out. Scotland Yard had tried to nobble the Police Complaints Authority. When Sir Cecil Clothier and his team returned for the fourth and final session, Gerry Bermingham was lying in wait for them.

He began carefully, as befitted a lawyer establishing his case. 'I believe that in December 1988 you issued a statement using the word "regret" in the circumstances of Mr Lundy's retirement?' Sir Cecil agreed and Bermingham struck. 'Am I right in understanding Deputy Commissioner John Dellow actually visited you in your headquarters?' The MP pressed harder. Was it the word 'regret' that they wanted deleted from the statement?

Yes, was the answer. Bermingham thrust home. 'I think it is right to say that they wanted the word "regret" out because it was a forceful statement from Sir Cecil?' Brigadier Pownall, sitting next to Clothier, agreed. 'I think you may well be right. They felt it was out of place, that word.' The press having long departed from Committee Room 15, there was nobody present to report the startling disclosure that the Yard had attempted to interfere with the independent watchdog. Later, Authority sources admitted that two senior officers, neither of which was Dellow, had turned up at their offices asking for the word 'regret' to be removed.

The committee deliberated and produced their recommendations. They began, 'Although it was our stated intention not to take up individual cases we could not discuss this subject without reference to the case of former Detective Superintendent Anthony Lundy.' The report continued, 'Tempting as it may be for a Force to be rid, and rid quickly, of an errant officer, there can be no justification in cases where serious offences are involved for using public funds to smooth that officer's departure before any serious discipline charges have been tried . . . Even greater anxiety than the inability to pursue the disciplinary charges was occasioned when Mr Lundy was filmed in extremely fit physical condition training for long-distance running in Metropolitan Police colours.'

Then followed the watchdog's prescription: 'We recommend that the Home Office should consult the appropriate police organisations with a view to establishing a board to review all applications for medical retirements of officers under disciplinary investigation.'

Parliament had no more to say about Tony Lundy.

The Home Office would prefer that the story ended there. So would Scotland Yard, which gives no sign of having learned any lessons: no apologies are offered, no questions permitted. No explanations are given about the bizarre relationship between the top detective and London's top criminal.

Garner was known to be a major criminal from the late 1960s yet the Yard seems unconcerned that it never caught him. Other detectives, lawyers and criminals saw that he was protected, a licensed gangster; the Yard leadership did not. When Garner was in trouble they rushed to his aid; secret letters pleading for soft treatment went to the judges in his VAT and passport trials. As he stood at the Old Bailey accused of a massive drugs conspiracy, senior Scotland Yard detectives effectively put his case — and all at public expense.

The quantity and quality of the warning signals about Lundy were devastating. From the late 1970s his simplistic sloganising about successes in the 'war against crime' should have alerted any thoughtful detective. The Yard in its vanity came to believe the headlines he created for the press.

It remains unbelievable that Lundy, ejected from the Flying Squad in 1980, could be brought back into sensitive intelligence areas. The leadership of the Yard, dazzled by Garner the 'best ever informant', lacked the capacity to foresee the scandals that would inevitably engulf them.

The discoveries of the Stagg team, the disclosures by supergrass Billy Young and the compromising pictures of Lundy with Garner, his old criminal partner Ross and Silver Bullion gunman Gibson were ignored. So too was the drip-feed of exposure in the tabloids, the quality press and finally the TV programmes.

But the Yard did not just bury its head in the sand; it went on the offensive. It gave Lundy a Good Conduct medal and suppressed the Steventon memo. It refused assistance, facilities, briefings, and guidance to inquisitive journalists. In early 1985 it mounted a whispering campaign that Harry Clement had gone crazy, tried to prosecute him for his disclosures, authorised the surveillance of Andrew Jennings, planted damaging stories in the press, intimidated the BBC and tried the same tactics on Granada TV.

The Yard was also petty and small-minded; in the spring of 1985 reporter Paul Lashmar, while working for the *Observer*, arranged a normal background briefing for a story he was writing about armed robbery. On the day of the meeting the Yard phoned to say the meeting was cancelled. Off the record, he was told, this was due to his 'track record'. That evening he went with his colleague David Leigh to be presented jointly with the 'Reporter of the Year' award.

Operation Albany was starved of resources, quietly closed down, re-opened under Parliamentary pressure, then run down secretly. When Garner was the target of a major criminal investigation he was able to see DAC Powis in secret. Later, Garner was able to meet DAC Worth when targeted simultaneously by Customs' Operation Redskin and the Yard's own Operation Distant Drum. The Stagg probe was delayed so long that everybody had their story ready and the trail was cold. Sergeant Miller avoided his discipline charges and left with an enhanced pension.

The story of 'The Untouchable' was eventually told, with the result the Yard most feared; an outside force was brought in to investigate. The Yard couldn't control it but it knew how to obstruct; it even accused the Yorkshire police of leaking the truth about the surveillance on Jennings, as if it was something that should be hidden.

It is a constitutional fiction that the Met is independent of the politicians. If the line were so clear-cut it would have been easy for the Select Committee to discover whether the Home Secretary was involved in the decision to let Lundy go.

Just how free the Met are to operate unchecked is shown by the number of civil servants dedicated to supervising Britain's biggest police force. Only eight bureaucrats in the Home Office police department, some quite junior, are responsible for scrutinising the activities of 30,000 employees at the Yard. They are not accessible to the public or the media and, when they surfaced before the Select Committee, had no comfort to offer a public whose confidence in the integrity of the Met has almost evaporated.

The Attorney General in 1988, who had the final say on whether

Lundy should be prosecuted, has his critics. It was depressing that he declined to allow the evidence about Lundy's leak to Mrs Garner or about the allegations over the supply of fencing by Salter to go before a jury of ordinary people. Earlier Attorney General Sir Michael Havers was deceived by the Met when they claimed that Operation Albany was still investigating Garner. No heads have rolled at the Yard over this humbug.

The Met, the Home Office and the politicians had failed the people and their lethargy protected the criminals; the only hope of justice lay with the Police Complaints Authority. Soon after its creation in 1985 the Authority optimistically added the word 'Independent' to its title. But the cards were always stacked against them; the 1984 Act that established the PCA denied them crucial powers.

When senior officers were under threat the Yard always knew it could beat it. As a last resort there would always be the option for suspect officers to disappear down the road of enhanced medical pensions. Since Lundy's departure there have been continual press reports of 'escapees', yet more officers being seen to get away with it.

The contempt in which the Met holds the Authority has been best illustrated by the departure, on the grounds of 'stress', of the marathon-running Lundy, who immediately recovered sufficiently to sell his story to the press and stand up to counsel in the Old Bailey witness box. The Met knew that there would be criticism; they also knew that there was no will anywhere to punish them for such an affront to justice and the public. Indeed the Met were so confident that they had no hesitation in telling the 'Independent' Complaints Authority to tone down their comments on Lundy's Christmas Eve departure.

No shock waves have registered in Parliament. The majority of politicians on both sides of the House have looked the other way. The Select Committee was cowed: the Yard's leadership hid behind the aura of the rank and file police officers who face danger daily; attack me, signalled Imbert, and you attack the men and women who risk their lives for you. Parliament was intimidated and duly obliged. Nobody ever drove the issues home.

It has been a 25-year saga and we have been tracking it for the last nine years. At the end, justice has been the first casualty. All but one of the main characters have moved on, unquestioned and untouched.

Garner has gone to a prison cell; he is a professional criminal but he alone of the cast list appears to have got his due desserts.

Ex-Superintendent Anthony Lundy has sold up and gone off to his new home in Spain with more money than most other retired detectives. Ringing in his ears is the question from conservative columnist Sir John Junor, who asked of Lundy's gold-plated goodbye, 'Doesn't it all smell a bit?'

Behind him Lundy has left men still serving long sentences on dubious evidence. Many of those men were convicted on nothing more than allegations from featherbedded supergrasses and confessions they claimed had been fabricated. They went to jail, Lundy made his name and Garner won his licence to rob.

The senior officer entrusted by the Yard to scrutinise the relationship between Garner and Lundy, ex-Commander Phil Corbett, has since retired. In November 1988 he wrote on the headed notepaper of his new employers, the Bank of England, declining to meet us. He added, 'I would be obliged if you would respect my decision to the extent of refraining to mention, at any stage, even your approach to me for assistance.'

Former Deputy Assistant Commissioner David Powis, from his job with the National Westminster Bank, also declined to talk.

His successor, Brian Worth, who now presents a TV crime show, met us but was reluctant to be interviewed.

Commissioner Imbert refused to talk to us and then briefed crime reporters that there was little new in our revelations about Lundy and Garner.

The people now have scant faith in the Metropolitan Police, whose priority is still to limit the damage rather than face up to abuses of power. The Yard does not envisage any basic reforms. It has however hired an expensive firm of image consultants to try and paint over the cracks.

Meanwhile, Special Agent Minto and Sergeant Bain have both retired. The German police and British Customs officers keep watch for Nikolaus Chrastny. Roy Garner sits in jail and ponders how he can trade his vast store of secret knowledge about police corruption for a reduced sentence. Tony Lundy suns himself in Spain.

ACKNOWLEDGMENTS

We owe many debts to the hundreds of people who have assisted us during the decade that it has taken to investigate this story.

Many people in public life have given us unstinting help and advice and it saddens us that if we gave them the individual thanks they deserve, their careers would be damaged.

In the same way many in the police service have thought it important to help us. Their motives were always the same: that the exposure of wrong-doing within their own ranks would in the long term help bring about a better and more responsive police force in London.

We wish to acknowledge the many fine and decent officers who have been outraged by what they saw going on about them. It is a sad comment on our society and our police tradition that the only way they could attempt to get justice done was to break the law and talk secretly with us.

We are happy to name the following people who have all made important contributions to discovering and developing this saga:

Colin Adams, Gordon Bain, Andy Bell, Gerry Bermingham MP, Roger Bolton, Mike Breece, Duncan Campbell of the *Guardian*, Harry Clement, Nick Davies, Tony Dawe, Walter Easy, Jeff Edwards, Michael Gillard, Paul Greengrass, Peter Jackson,

David Jervis, David Leigh, Mike Minto, Claire Powell, Chris Price, James Saunders, Martin Short, Clive Soley MP, Chris Smith MP and John Ware.

Our greatest debt of thanks must go to Ray Fitzwalter and Granada Television. The guidance and commitment from which we have benefited over the years was vital. Without that support this story might never have been told.

We also thank those close to us who have coped patiently while we have devoted so much time to this work.

Andrew Jennings,
Paul Lashmar
and Vyv Simson
May 1990